BIKE SCOT- LAND TRAILS GUIDE

The authors and publisher have made every effort to ensure that the information in this publication is accurate, and accept no responsibility whatsoever for any loss, injury or inconvenience experienced by any person or persons whilst using this book.

published by
pocket mountains ltd
6 Church Wynd, Bo'ness EH51 0AN
www.pocketmountains.com

ISBN: 0-9550822-2-6
EAN: 978-0-95508-222-1

A catalogue record for this book is available from the British Library

All route maps are based on 1945 Popular Edition Ordnance Survey material and revised from field surveys by Pocket Mountains Ltd, 2006. © Pocket Mountains Ltd 2006.

Printed in Poland

Introduction

In late 2005 the International Mountain Bicycling Association (IMBA) declared Scotland the number one place in the world for mountain biking and predicted that it will retain its Global Superstar status for years to come.

Some were surprised that Scotland had crept up on and then leapfrogged destinations like British Columbia, Colorado and the Alps, but mountain biking has developed in this country at a pace that is unmatched by any other nation.

In fact, the mountain biking picture in Scotland is changing at such a rate that new routes are emerging all the time which means that our Trails Guide, while setting out to be comprehensive, does not pretend to be definitive.

Included among the 40 routes in this book are all of the main centres, or the places that have become recognised hubs of the sport, but you will also find a selection of the unusual, remote and bizarre.

Not everyone, for example, will be excited by the idea of throwing their precious mountain bike into a boat to be deposited in Tarbet, a remote settlement on the North Morar peninsula, in order to ride a narrow 11km trail that clings precariously to hills whose slopes plunge into Britain's deepest freshwater loch – but others surely will.

Selecting 'the best' can never be an exact science, of course, but – from the man-made trails at Glentress, which have provided many thousands with an introduction to the intoxicating thrill of singletrack riding, to the aforementioned Tarbet route or the natural trails that exist on the Hebridean island of Harris – we think we've come up with a list that will be pretty near the best in many riders' books.

That said, there are one or two notable omissions from this guide. These include the Dark Side at Mabie, with its technical North Shore, and the downhill tracks at Innerleithen and Fort William, since we felt that technical trials-style mountain biking, even downhill riding, would detract from our main focus on cracking cross-country rides.

Cross-country mountain biking is one of the most inclusive sports around, with enthusiasts drawn from all walks of life and age groups. At the same time, a lot of dedicated mountain biking trails do demand a reasonable level of riding competence. In our selection of waymarked trails, we have made particular reference to red- and black-graded routes and among our choice of wild routes a number are also very challenging.

This is not intended to exclude the newcomer from enjoying Scotland's wild or waymarked trails, since riding competence can be built up through experience, particularly if you start off on easier green- and blue-graded trails (also offered at many of the dedicated centres highlighted in this guide) or by taking lessons, such as those that are available at Glentress.

Roots of mountain biking

When mountain bikes first appeared, in the late 1970s – reputedly in Marin County, California – they bore little relation to what you see today. Suspension systems, hydraulic disc brakes and indexed gearing, to name just three technical innovations, were some years away. So was the twisting, gnarly, technical singletrack that is so popular today.

It must have started, though, with somebody riding on tight, narrow paths, and finding the experience to be utterly exhilarating. How better to describe the sensation? It's adrenaline-fuelled, a buzz, a thrill and a lot of fun – but sheer exhilaration is the description that most aptly sums up the feeling of riding the best mountain bike trails.

The sport has come a long way since the mountain bike first appeared on the market and the pioneers began riding in places that had previously been out of bounds to cyclists. Obviously, there are still lots of natural singletrack trails – quite a few are featured in this guide – but there is also an enviable network of official centres with dedicated, man-made trails designed and built with mountain bikers in mind.

There is nothing random or haphazard about such trails: in most cases they are the result of several years of study and experience, many hours of planning, and a lot of painstaking work to realise the designs of the trailbuilder.

As one trailbuilder puts it, 'it's about imagining what sort of buzz you might get through riding in a particular place, and so you think: what kind of trail can make that happen? Whether it's a massive adrenaline rush, or a real technical challenge, it's all about designing an experience. And it's a much harder, more laborious process than most people think'.

The story in Scotland

Scotland's thriving mountain biking scene has its roots at Glentress in the Tweed Valley. Work began there in Spring 2000 on the forest's first singletrack, designed by 'trailbuilding guru' Pete Laing. The first route established at Glentress formed the basis for the red route that is still arguably Scotland's most popular trail today.

It was not long after the official opening of this route that Britain was hit by the foot and mouth outbreak which meant that the countryside was effectively closed. Glentress was one of the first Forestry Commission Scotland forests to re-open, and its popularity indicated a hitherto unknown demand for mountain biking.

This led to the ambitious 7Stanes initiative to build seven mountain biking centres across southern Scotland, largely as a response to the impact of foot and mouth on the local economy.

The establishment of

dedicated centres has expanded beyond its heartland in the Southern Uplands to the Central Belt (Carron Valley), the North (Fort William, Laggan, Black Isle, Moray), and the North-east (Kirkhill).

Many are works in progress, others are still being planned. What it all means is that the sport is buzzing in Scotland, and there are no signs of it slowing down. On the contrary, there is a sense among mountain bikers in Scotland that the IMBA recognition heralded the start, not the end, of the revolution.

Access and the environment

Following the publication of the Land Reform (Scotland) Act, it is generally believed that Scotland has the finest access arrangements in Europe, if not the world. The public now has the right to be on most land for recreation, and that includes mountain bikers, but under the new legislation the right of access depends on whether it is exercised responsibly. The Scottish Outdoor Access Code sets out many responsibilities which are pretty much common sense, including leaving gates as you find them and taking litter home with you, but there are additional responsibilities for cyclists. On paths and tracks shared with other users, walkers and horse riders have the right of way: you should give advance warning of your presence and dismount and walk where shared paths are narrow. Take care not to alarm farm animals and wildlife. If cycling off-path, particularly in winter, try to avoid wet, boggy or soft ground and churning up the surface, and use purpose-built tracks and paths where they exist.

Glossary

MTB abbreviation for a mountain bike

Hard tail bike with no rear suspension

Full suss bike with front and rear suspension

Singletrack the ultimate mountain bike riding experience: trails not much wider than your tyres

Fun park sections of downhill singletrack where features such as jumps, tabletops, doubles, berms, etc. come thick and fast

Chicken run a little section of trail, usually off to the side of a jump or drop-off, that provides an alternative to the scary stuff

Rock garden rocks embedded in the ground to provide a bone-jarring ride

Berm a steeply banked corner, built up to allow riders to corner at speed

Drop-off a sheer drop, which can either be jumped or – providing it's not too severe – rolled over, dropping the front wheel first

Bombhole a steep drop into a hole, followed by a steep climb back out

Rock steps varying sizes, usually a single step uphill

Doubles two jumps, like camel bumps, one immediately after the other

Tabletop like a double but with the middle bit filled in to leave a flat top suitable either for rolling over or jumping, to land on the down side

Roots Tree roots: a common obstacle on the trails in Scotland. And potentially hazardous as they can be very slippy

North Shore raised timber trails which appear at a number of centres in Scotland. They owe their name to their Canadian origins, where they are used to cross wet or boggy ground.

Tips and tricks

- On steep or technical descents, stand on the pedals, absorbing bumps with knees
- Keep your centre of gravity as low as possible, even when standing on the pedals
- Look ahead: keep your eyes as far up the trail as possible
- Don't focus on obstacles: keep your eyes trained on the best line around them
- Change gear before you need to, especially on the approach to a climb
- On steep descents, keep your weight back to make the front end of the bike as light as possible
- Don't hang off the back of the saddle if that locks the arms: straight arms make it impossible to absorb bumps or control the bike
- Use both brakes: the front brake has about 70 per cent more stopping power, but 'feathering' both is the best way to maintain control
- The most efficient way to climb is in the saddle: only stand up when the slope is so steep that you need more leverage on the pedals
- When climbing out of the saddle, keep your weight over the back wheel
- To negotiate big roots or step-ups, transfer your weight from the back to the front of the bike
- Entering a switchback, slow down, take a wide approach and aim for the inside line as you hit the apex
- Lean into corners: try to let your body flow with the trail
- Never brake abruptly on the approach to a drop-off, even if you think you're going too fast
- Pull a gentle wheelie as you approach the edge of a drop-off: landing on both wheels is the best way to absorb the shock
- When airborne make sure arms and legs are bent, ready for landing
- Go easy with the jet spray on the moving parts of your bike, especially the suspension system.

Riding safely

The most obvious and important safety tip is to wear a helmet. Always. And wear a good one, approved by ANSI and SNELL. Cost is a guide to quality, though it isn't the only consideration: it is best, however, to avoid the cheapest models on the market.

Something to be aware of, too, is that helmets made of compressed polystyrene do have a lifespan. It might be three, five, six years: check the manufacturer's manual and replace the helmet when they recommend. For this reason, never buy a second-hand helmet.

Elbow and knee pads are also increasingly popular, and not just among downhill specialists. They can certainly protect the joints from injury if you crash, though some riders find them uncomfortable and restrictive on cross-country rides. Some feel, too, that body armour might lull riders into a false sense of security, so it's important to remember that, in the event of a serious crash, this would only really prevent superficial injuries. The best advice, no matter what you're wearing, is to ride within your limits.

Trail grading

At all of the mountain biking centres featured in this guide, trails are graded according to difficulty and the grading system below is generally recognised. In all cases, though, the weather, the quality of your bike and the ability of your companions can change the difficulty of a route.

Green – easy: suitable for beginners and families on mountain bikes. Mostly level terrain with shallow climbs and descents on usually hardened surfaces but may be loose, uneven and muddy

Blue – moderate: suitable for intermediate-level riders with basic off-road skills on mountain bikes. Moderate gradients, with possible short steep sections and obstacles such as rocks and roots

Red – difficult: suitable for competent mountain bikers with good off-road skills on better-quality mountain bikes with recommended front suspension (forks). Steeper, tougher climbs and drops with berms, boardwalks, steps, large stones, possible water crossings and cambers. Varied surface 0.4m+ wide

Black – severe: suitable for expert riders with a high level of fitness and stamina on good-quality mountain bikes with front suspension. Extended steep sections; large steps and drop-offs. Varied but always challenging surface with prolonged rocky/loose sections

'Double diamond' black – very severe: suitable for technically expert riders with jumping ability on good-quality mountain bikes (dual suspension system). Extreme exposure/risk; severe drops and steep inclines; may include 'downhill'-style sections, very narrow gaps and North Shore.

Kitbag essentials

- A water bottle or camelbak, allowing around 500ml fluid for every hour of the ride. Don't wait until you are thirsty or fatigued as this means you are already dehydrated: start before or early on in the ride and continue to take several sips every 10-15 minutes. Always thoroughly clean your water bottle or camelbak after your ride.
- Carbohydrate or sugar-loaded food, such as bananas, energy bars, flapjacks or gel sachets, for any prolonged cycling (more than an hour)
- Sports drinks (you can make your own by adding one-third of a teaspoon of salt and up to five tablespoons of sugar per litre of water) can provide the carbohydrate and fluid you need
- A multi tool with chain link extractor: removing a link from the chain can be the difference between riding home and having to walk for miles
- Cable ties: simple, but can provide a (temporary) solution to numerous mechanical mishaps
- Pump, tyre levers, two spare tubes plus a puncture repair kit
- Mobile phone (but remote locations may have no reception)
- A light waterproof
- Map, if you're riding an unmarked route (and a compass on hill routes)
- First aid kit: compact first aid kits for cyclists are available but it's just as easy to make your own.

The south of Scotland has to be
designated the spiritual home of Scottish
mountain biking, since the Borders and
Dumfries & Galloway are really where it
all started.

Specifically, it was here that the 7Stanes
initiative was born, and this has meant that
the area has now become not just the best
place in Scotland, but one of the top
destinations for cross-country mountain
biking in the world.

The 7Stanes project was led by Forestry
Commission Scotland alongside eight
partners, including local councils and
enterprise companies. Together they
pledged £1m, a sum that was matched
by European structural funding, and that
led to the development of the seven
centres, at Ae, Dalbeattie, Glentrool,
Kirroughtree, Mabie, Newcastleton and

Tweed Valley (Glentress and Innerleithen).

These centres boast the highest quality
singletrack, in terms of construction and
design. Only at Glentrool is this not the case
– instead of singletrack it has a long-
distance touring route – but at the other
centres there are miles of flowing and, in
places, technically challenging trails.

They're known as the 7Stanes because
each venue features a 'stane' – the Scots
word for stone – hidden somewhere in
the forest.

As well as the 7Stanes centres there are
other places to explore, including longer
rides that link up some of the centres.
A route through Gypsy Glen offers a great
alternative to the centres, for example, while
at Drumlanrig there are natural singletrack
trails that are completely different in
character to what you'll find at the 7Stanes.

Southern Scotland

Glentress Red

Distance **19km waymarked (Red)**
Map **OS Explorer 337** Facilities **Car park (fee), bike shop/hire/lessons/night riding, café, toilets, showers, bike wash**

Glentress is the undisputed mecca for mountain bikers in Scotland and, since the 19km red route is by far the most popular trail here, this in turn makes it the most popular in Scotland and possibly the UK.

Like all five trails in this forest, which 's in the Tweed Valley, 3km east of the ders town of Peebles, the red route from the lower car park, where you'll d the Hub in the Forest café and

slog up the forest road is broken ur on to the first section of k, which is undulating but mainly gotiating a path through the trees.

Then it's back on to the forest road, and up to the Buzzard's Nest car park, an alternative start point for those using the 1.5km skills loop, which is ideal for beginners, or the revamped freeride area above the car park.

Onwards and upwards, past the entrance to the freeride area, and finally you're at the start of the first bit of downhill singletrack – Pennel's Vennel. Arguably this is as technical as any of the sections around the course, with roots, a small water splash, steep drops and a few strategically placed rocks providing the challenges before the trail levels out and leads on to a meandering uphill stretch of singletrack.

This rises in hairpins to the viewpoint, with its picnic table providing an attractive spot for a breather, before snaking up through the trees, with some tight turns, to meet a higher forest road. After skirting the

side of the hill, with great views across the Tweed Valley, the climb continues in switchbacks through Spooky Wood.

Eventually you emerge at the highest point of the red trail, and another excellent viewpoint, which doubles as the gateway to a section that, since it opened, has proved a magnet for mountain bikers throughout the country. Spooky Wood, the fun park-style descent, has been compared to a BMX track: it's smooth, it flows and in its 1.5km it packs in no fewer than 18 jumps, 17 tabletops, four rock drops and twelve 180-degree bermed bends.

This section tends to divide people, though it is probably fair to point out that there are more fans than detractors. Some love its smooth, flowing lines and BMX-style features, others prefer their mountain biking a little rougher and more ragged. But while there are plenty of trails like this in Glentress, there is nowhere else quite like Spooky Wood in Scotland, at least not on this scale.

After Spooky Wood it is virtually downhill all the way. The trail continues through more established, rugged and rocky sections of trail – the big dipper style Hit Squad Hill, The Matrix and Magic Mushroom, all established favourites for many riders.

Finally, Sair Fecht deposits you back on the forest road where it all started, with a 300m uphill slog before the final singletrack descent of Falla Brae.

Less challenging than the red route are two blue options of 8km and 14km, which include some nice singletrack while missing out Spooky Wood. The pièce de résistance is Electric Blue, a flowing singletrack descent that swoops down from the Buzzard's Nest car park to the opening to Falla Brae. Then it's back to the Hub for some great post-ride nosh.

Glentress Helly Hansen V-Trail

Distance **29km waymarked (Black)**
Map **OS Explorer 337** Facilities **Car park (fee), bike shop/hire/lessons/night riding, café, toilets, showers, bike wash**

The Helly Hansen V-Trail has a completely different feel to the red and blue routes at Glentress. While these are relatively compact and very attractive to a diverse weekend crowd, the longer, more rugged black trail represents a big step up.

The starting point is the same — the lower car park by the Hub — and it makes its ascent along the forest road, with the same singletrack detour, all the way up to the Buzzard's Nest car park.

Here it diverges, avoiding Pennel's Vennel to head straight out along the forest road to the first stretch of black-graded singletrack: a rough and rocky section known as Soor Plooms. As it enters the forest, the trail rises

steadily, giving a bone-jarring ride before it finally brings you out on another forest road that leads on to singletrack section number two: The Goat Track.

Like Soor Plooms, this is an evocative and appropriate name. The trail here becomes more technical, with abrupt drop-offs, rock steps and even a stone chute, which is as potentially hazardous as it sounds.

These sections are quite different to the exhilarating singletrack descents that characterise the red route. They are more undulating and technically challenging. Full concentration is required.

But for the next section it is not concentration but stamina that is needed: Tower Ride is a shared and torturously steep path that rises in a straight line to the opening to The Kipps Loop, a climb that lasts for 2.5km but can seem like it is going on forever and ever. And ever.

The Kipps Loop trail is rugged and rocky,

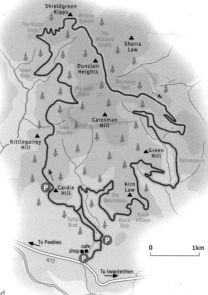

snaking across and up the hill and taking you on to an exposed ridge before climbing to a viewpoint with a hut, a handy place to stop, admire the scenery and recover.

Make the most of it: there's more climbing ahead. Leaving the shelter and cresting the hill brings you out at a welcome section of downhill singletrack but at the bottom the only way is up again, this time on a trail known as Britney Spears (Hit Me Baby One More Time). Yes, just when you thought the summit of The Kipps Loop was as high as it got, there's more.

Britney Spears takes you up to the Mustard Snake, the final steep climb up to the mast at the summit of Dunslair Heights. Now it's on to The Boundary Trail, an undulating and fairly challenging stretch of singletrack that dips in and out of the forest before joining Shane McGowan, which is rocky and steep in places with lots of loose stones. The trail curls round Green Hill and descends to the forest road.

Deliverance is the forbidding-sounding 5km singletrack loop that drops from here into the glen before climbing again – it is hard going, especially at this stage of the ride. Eventually it delivers you to Ewok Village where sections of North Shore and a see-saw might be a step too far for some, but these features provide a good

test of bike handling skills and balance.

More technical downhill follows in the form of Black Dog, with its big steps and drop-offs and more North Shore, and the Wormhole, a tight, dark trail that burrows into the forest after a treacherously steep and rocky entrance.

There is no let-up on the V-Trail. Initial sections of rocky trail, followed by long, exposed climbs, followed by draining classic cross-country trails finished off with technical downhill. No matter how fit and competent you are, this route proves a real challenge.

13

Innerleithen Traquair XC

Distance **19km waymarked (Red and Black)**
Map **OS Explorer 337** Facilities **Car park (fee), toilets on site, bike shop/hire in Innerleithen, uplift service from Glentress**

Traquair XC is a technically challenging red- and black- graded cross-country route that owes its rollercoaster finish to Innerleithen's downhill tradition.

Innerleithen is one of the UK's best known venues for downhill mountain biking, with a lot of work having gone into building serious tracks, and a well-established uplift service in operation. There are more plans to continue to improve its credentials as the country's hub for downhilling, while the emphasis at Glentress, also in the Tweed Valley, remains focused on the cross-country side of the sport.

But as a 7Stanes centre (somewhat confusingly Glentress and Innerleithen are bracketed together as Tweed Valley) there is also a very good 19km cross-country route, Traquair XC, at Innerleithen. In terms of length and difficulty it is somewhere between the red and black routes at Glentress, and as such offers a refreshing change, with a whopping 90 per cent of the trail reckoned to be singletrack.

It will extend those who consider the Glentress red route to be their limit, however, with some of the later downhill sections at Innerleithen possibly proving a challenge too far. It gets pretty technical, and a couple of the sections have been upgraded from a red to a black grading to reflect that.

The Traquair cross-country route starts from the Red Bull Project Downhill centre, where all the downhill tracks finish, and

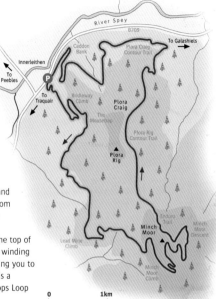

you're straight on to a great singletrack climb that snakes up the hill, beginning an extended ascent that eventually takes you to 570m and the summit of Minch Moor.

Before you reach the high, exposed moor, the trail alternates between singletrack and wider bridleways, taking you deep into Traquair forest. The singletrack is quite gnarly in places, with roots and rocks: even here it is a grade up from challenges posed by the red route at Glentress.

In total it's a 6km-plus slog to the top of Minch Moor, with nice singletrack winding up through the heather and exposing you to all the elements at the summit. It's a serious climb, not dissimilar to Kipps Loop at Glentress, and a rewarding one.

At the top comes the main prize, though, with the trail cutting immediately and steeply downhill via a series of big berms and swooping singletrack. Best not to let this fast section lull you into a false sense of security, however, because there's still a tough climb to come. The path eventually bottoms out and then simply veers straight back up, over ground that can be spongy and heavy going.

Then in the second half of the ride come the black-graded sections of singletrack. First is Plora Craig, which drops down the hill by way of some rugged, steep and rocky singletrack. This catches lots of riders out: it

requires decent balance and bike handling skills, and the consequences of misjudging some sections could be quite nasty.

Caddon Bank takes you back on to more traditionally flowing downhill, though again it has its challenges. This final section of singletrack owes something to the downhill tradition at Innerleithen, being a 2km rollercoaster of a trail, with big jumps, rock steps and drop-offs, a huge bombhole and a succession of enormous bermed corners.

For Glentress regulars, the Traquair XC route represents something a bit different – and it's nowhere near as busy.

15

The Gypsy Glen

Distance **50km unmarked**
Map **OS Landranger 73 or OS Explorer 337**
Facilities **Pubs, shops, cafés in Peebles and Innerleithen**

This offers an alternative big day out high up in the heart of Scotland's most popular mountain biking country.

The Tweed Valley houses the outstanding mountain biking centres of Innerleithen and Glentress, but for anyone wanting a change from the many miles of man-made trails that make this area the pre-eminent mountain biking venue in Scotland, there are some interesting alternatives as well as opportunities to link the two centres.

A particularly good ride involves traversing the tops of the rolling hills that separate Innerleithen from Peebles, and Glentress, on opposite sides of the Tweed Valley.

From Innerleithen, follow the minor road towards Yarrow Valley, across the bridge over the River Tweed, with the mountain bike centre on your left, and continue on to Traquair. After Traquair there's a small road to the right, taking you into an estate and a road that gradually deteriorates from tarmac to dirt track to virtually no track at all.

And this is when the mountain biking begins. The track snakes through the valley, alongside the river, before the hills rear up in front of you. There are bits where the path disappears, but eventually there's a river crossing, followed by the steep ascent of Stake Law, where there are only traces of path, most of them petering out after a few metres. Zigzagging is the best, or only, method by which to negotiate a hill that can be quite boggy, particularly at the bottom.

The target is the good quality drove road that cuts across the hill and, turning right once you reach it, takes you on up to the summit with its cairn and fantastic panoramic views of the area. The drove road is undulating, rocky and steep in places, and it covers an area known as Gypsy Glen – which refers to the route from Peebles South through to St Mary's Loch.

From the summit of Stake Law, Peebles is usually clearly visible, nestling six miles (10km) away (a signpost tells you as much). It doesn't look 10km, and doesn't feel it, either, because the ride from here to the town is fast and exhilarating – even though it isn't quite downhill all the way.

Parts of this descent are glorious: exposed grassy hillside, where just about any line is possible. With few obstacles, it can be very, very fast if you let go (but watch out for walkers).

Peebles makes a good refreshment stop, before the tough final segment of the ride, dipping into Glentress. Coming out of Peebles on the Innerleithen road it's best not to head all the way to the Glentress car park, but instead to ride up the steep climb of Janet's Brae – also known locally as Jenny's Brae. In places this is a real slog, with the feel of an Alpine pass as it climbs in switchbacks.

Finally, this brings you out at the Glentress trails, by the skills loop. From here you can join the red, blue or even – for the very keen – black trails, or alternatively it's possible to follow the forest road that curls round the valley to Deliverance. Down Deliverance, just before the trail starts to rise, there's a sneaky little left turn which follows a vague path. This brings you out at Horsburgh farm, between Glentress and Innerleithen, and from there it's just 5km by road back to Innerleithen.

17

Drumlanrig Red and Black

Distance **24km waymarked (Red and Black)**
Maps **OS Explorer 321 and 329**
Facilities **Car park (estate entry fee), bike shop/hire, café, toilets, showers, bike wash**

Drumlanrig provides a unique mountain biking experience on tight all-natural trails which weave the length and breadth of this privately owned country park.

The mountain biking trails in the grounds of Drumlanrig Castle are the kind that you find all over Scotland – natural little paths that weave intricately through the forest. Great fun to ride, but often difficult to make a proper ride out of, since it's impossible to know where they end up – or if they go anywhere at all.

Unless, that is, they happen to be waymarked. And in Drumlanrig they are, giving you options of riding for up to 24km in this stunning estate, virtually all on

these delightful, testing and very natural seeming trails.

They are essentially natural – in the sense that they are not surfaced with imported stones or grit – but they've also been hand-crafted and 'organically grown' by Rik Allsop, who established a lot of the early trails in nearby Mabie forest. These trails are resilient and, as long as they're ridden, will stand the test of time. Some also have a more solid base, thanks to the discovery, while the trails were being built, of old footpaths, partially buried now but constructed over a century ago by the 80 or so pathbuilders employed by the estate.

Rik runs a bike shop in the courtyard of the castle, which includes a number of other shops and a tearoom, as well as a cycling museum dedicated to Drumlanrig-based blacksmith Kirkpatrick MacMillan who, in 1839, in the nearby village of Keir, built what is now acknowledged to have been the world's first bike. So Drumlanrig can make some claim to being the home of cycling.

It is a privately owned estate, belonging to the Duke of Buccleuch, making the support and development of mountain biking all the more unusual, and welcome. As well as the trails themselves, Drumlanrig Castle has also become a regular venue for cross-country racing, using Rik's trails.

These bear the trailbuilder's signature: tight and twisting with literally thousands of roots and branches and other natural obstacles to negotiate. But it is not all fiddly; there are also fast, sweeping descents here.

Within metres of leaving the courtyard, the red route shoots off the main path and burrows into the trees.
The trails are all well signposted but after a few kilometres you have to decide whether to continue on the red (a 15.5km loop, but with plenty of shortcuts back to base) or opt for the black, which adds an extra 8km.

What all of the trails have in common are roots. Riding over them requires a particular skill and one that demands practice, but at Drumlanrig you have no choice.

The trail weaves an intricate route through the forest, and skirts around open hillside, passing several small lochs, with forays into deep bombholes, over log jumps and up steep but short-lived technical climbs or longer hairpins. It is this sheer variety that makes the experience of riding Drumlanrig such a constant and exhilarating challenge: it is simply not possible to ride here without full concentration.

It offers a very different experience to the neighbouring 7Stanes centres – Ae, Mabie and Dalbeattie are all very close by car – but Drumlanrig rates as a hugely enjoyable ride.

Wanlockhead Gold Rush

Distance **52km unmarked**
Map **OS Landranger 78** Facilities **Car park
(entry fee), bike shop/hire, café, toilets,
showers, bike wash at Drumlanrig Castle,
shop, pub, café, hostel at Wanlockhead**

**There's gold in them thar hills on this
epic ride in the mineral-rich Lowthers,
taking in Britain's highest village and
part of the Southern Upland Way.**

This corner of Scotland is as well served for
mountain bike trails as anywhere in the
world, but there is more to it than the
waymarked trails of the Drumlanrig estate,
Ae, Mabie, Dalbeattie and Kirroughtree –
fantastic though they are.

From the grounds of Drumlanrig Castle it
is possible to embark on a real adventure

– a 52km humdinger of a ride that involves
a lot of climbing, followed by a long and
very rewarding descent from Britain's
highest village back to Drumlanrig.

The first part even takes in some of those
waymarked trails in the estate, along roughly
half of the red route until the section known
as Dr Evil. At this switchback in the trail you
break away from the red route and follow the
River Nith, heading north.

The trail comes and goes a little along
the valley floor, but it's all rideable and the
path does continue: just keep riding parallel
to the bank of the river. At Burnmouth, it
becomes more grassy and muddy until you
join the singletrack road.

Follow this northwest for around 5km,
over Eliok Bridge and on to the main A76,

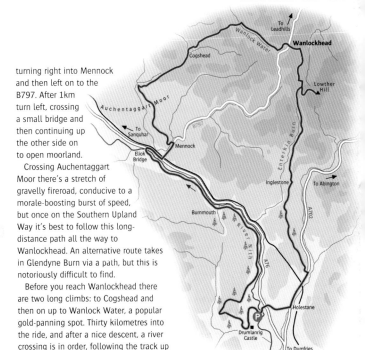

turning right into Mennock and then left on to the B797. After 1km turn left, crossing a small bridge and then continuing up the other side on to open moorland.

Crossing Auchentaggart Moor there's a stretch of gravelly fireroad, conducive to a morale-boosting burst of speed, but once on the Southern Upland Way it's best to follow this long-distance path all the way to Wanlockhead. An alternative route takes in Glendyne Burn via a path, but this is notoriously difficult to find.

Before you reach Wanlockhead there are two long climbs: to Cogshead and then on up to Wanlock Water, a popular gold-panning spot. Thirty kilometres into the ride, and after a nice descent, a river crossing is in order, following the track up to Wanlockhead, where the shop and Museum of Lead Mining café provide timely refreshment stops.

Just because you've reached Britain's highest village doesn't mean an end to the climbing. Still higher is Lowther Hill but it's virtually all downhill from here. First there's a steep grassy path by the side of the Enterkin Burn. Apart from one or two boggy bits this is an excellent descent, combining grassy trail with gravel-covered, narrow singletrack. At the bottom and with 40km

in your legs by now, there's a sharp left turn and a strength-sapping ascent until the first switchback, where a right turn takes you on another grassy track, dropping down to Ingelstone.

Then it's on to the road, following the A702 for 2km to Holestane before turning into the grounds of the estate to be met by the magnificent – and by this point very welcome – sight of Drumlanrig Castle.

Glentrool Big Country Ride

Distance 58km waymarked but ungraded
Maps OS Explorer 319 or OS Landranger 77
and 83 Facilities Shop, café, toilets at
Glentrool Visitor Centre

**It's stamina rather than technical ability
that's a must for this testing, but
ultimately very rewarding, 7Stanes ride.**

Glentrool is the odd one out of the
7Stanes centres – an epic, old-style ride
along minor forest roads. What makes it
unique among the centres is that there is
no singletrack, not a metre of it.

Singletrack addicts, therefore, might like
to head for nearby Kirroughtree instead. But
for those who like touring, and exploring a
remote corner of Southern Scotland,
Glentrool is an attractive proposition. It's
also fully waymarked, which will appeal to
those who have become used to the
7Stanes signposts which ensure you don't
get lost in any of the other centres.

The challenge at Glentrool is in the
length. At 58km, it is a serious distance,

and it is also undulating, with big, long
climbs, the toughest of which comes,
inconveniently enough, at 40km. Most will
be on their last legs by this stage, making
it even tougher. And there are no shortcuts.
It is a testing ride and estimates for the
time needed to complete it range from five
to nine hours – a long day in the saddle.

But it is stunning. The route explores a
large area of the Galloway Forest Park,
Britain's largest forest park. When it was
originally opened in 1947 the 25,000
hectares of open hill and forest was
designated Glentrool National Forest Park,
but it was renamed Galloway Forest Park in
1997, by which time it comprised 76,000
hectares of sweeping hills and forests, and
remote, unspoilt Galloway landscape.

The trail head is at the Glentrool Visitor
Centre, which sits in a beautiful little
clearing by the Water of Minnoch, with
picnic tables by the river. Other, shorter
mountain bike routes are possible in the
forest, and maps are available, but the

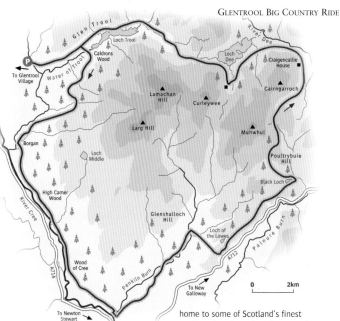

7Stanes ride is marked out by those familiar signs.

By a combination of very minor roads and well-established forest tracks it follows the Water of Trool to the foot of Loch Trool, turning right over the river and heading south towards Newton Stewart. The first climb takes you up to a cairn before dropping down to Borgan. The track skirts forests, with High Camer Wood turning into Wood of Cree, and runs parallel to, but high above, the main A714 road.

Just short of the town, the track almost doubles back on itself, following the Penkiln Burn towards Kirroughtree, the forest that is home to some of Scotland's finest singletrack trails. Before then you climb towards Glenshalloch Hill and then enter Kirroughtree forest, riding on tracks that are tantalisingly close to the singletrack trails – but it's probably impractical to enjoy any diversion on to these at this point.

The track continues up to Loch of the Lowes, running parallel to the A712, before climbing to Black Loch and Poultrybuie Hill, then heading on to Munwhul, and along the River Dee to Craigencallie House. Riding by Loch Dee, and around the White Laggan Bothy, takes you to Glenhead Burn, which leads up to Glenhead and then through Glen Trool, passing Loch Trool just before the visitor centre.

23

Kirroughtree Black Craigs

Distance **29km waymarked (Red and Black)**
Map **OS Explorer 319** Facilities **Shop, café,
toilets at Kirroughtree Visitor Centre**

**Hailed by many as the finest of the
7Stanes centres, Kirroughtree contains
miles of epic singletrack.**

Since it opened, this centre has attained
something approaching cult status. It could
be because, of all the 7Stanes, it seems like
the most remote, challenging and unusual
in terms of landscape and the forests it
explores. It also has a devoted and growing
band of admirers. A lot of mountain bikers,
when asked their favourite place to ride,
will respond 'Kirroughtree'.

What makes it unique among the 7Stanes
centres is its sense of wilderness and scale.
Even if it isn't far from the popular trails at
Dalbeattie and Mabie, pedal out of the car
park on any of the four routes – from the
beginners' Bargaly Wood, a 6km green-
graded route, to the red-graded 14km

Twister Trail or Black Craigs, the epic 29km
black route (which incorporates the Twister
Trail) – and you will feel like you are
venturing well off the beaten track.

There are 43km of singletrack trails at
Kirroughtree, and they bear the 7Stanes
hallmark of imaginative design and quality
construction, as well as utterly thrilling and
in places quite technical riding. They are well
built and hard wearing, too, with the earth
and granite surface augmented by imported
black shale, which gives them a distinctive
appearance as well as ride quality.

Black Craigs is a 15km add-on to the red
Twister Trail, which means that you can
keep your options open depending on what
shape the legs are in. The early sections of
red singletrack are indicative of what is to
follow, though in terms of difficulty they
provide a relatively gentle introduction.
They flow nicely through the forest with the
odd rock obstacle to negotiate and the
climbs of Doon Hill and The White Witch.

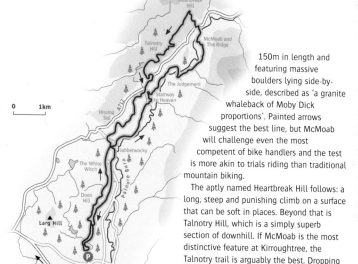

150m in length and featuring massive boulders lying side-by-side, described as 'a granite whaleback of Moby Dick proportions'. Painted arrows suggest the best line, but McMoab will challenge even the most competent of bike handlers and the test is more akin to trials riding than traditional mountain biking.

The aptly named Heartbreak Hill follows: a long, steep and punishing climb on a surface that can be soft in places. Beyond that is Talnotry Hill, which is a simply superb section of downhill. If McMoab is the most distinctive feature at Kirroughtree, the Talnotry trail is arguably the best. Dropping off the hill, it swoops and twists initially down open hillside before entering the forest. There are some seriously big steps and drop-offs here which can catch you unawares. Talnotry is conducive to speed but, until you know the trail and what lies ahead, it is better to proceed with a little caution.

After more quality singletrack, including Hissing Syd, you re-join the red-graded singletrack, which provides undulating riding – this can be technical in places, and also draining at this late stage of the ride – all the way back to Kirroughtree Visitor Centre.

There is also a taster loop near the car park, and the blue Larg Hill ride, which shares some of the red trail, with a 4km Doon Hill extension, is well worth exploring.

Switching from The Twister to Black Craigs, the trail moves on to some very technical climbing, with Stairway to Heaven followed by The Judgement, both jaggedly rocky and tricky in places, with step-ups and other obstacles.

You continue on singletrack and remote fireroads, with views of the Galloway hills, and then, near to the furthest point, comes Kirroughtree's most talked about feature.

Leaving the fireroad you enter a giant boulderfield. This is McMoab, an obstacle course for mountain biking, measuring

Dalbeattie Hardrock

Distance **27km waymarked (Red with optional Black features)**
Map **OS Landranger 84 or Explorer 313**
Facilities **Pub, shop, café in Dalbeattie**

A 7Stanes classic with hard, granite-based singletrack trails and some technically challenging features.

Dalbeattie was one of the first of Forestry Commission Scotland's 7Stanes centres to open, and from day one it proved popular. It also has a unique feature that continues to draw mountain bikers from all over – namely, The Slab.

This is a 12m-long slab of granite that drops almost vertically – or that's how it appears from the top. Groups of mountain bikers tend to gather above The Slab, like surfers waiting for the next big wave. In their case, though, it is usually to peer anxiously down and debate whether or not to ride it. The consequences of taking the wrong line, or losing your nerve and touching the brakes halfway down, could be painful.

But The Slab is just one feature at Dalbeattie, and it is not compulsory: there is a nice singletrack detour. And, in fact, this is a very good centre for a range of abilities, with a skills loop near the start ideal for novices or for a quick warm up.

The defining characteristic of the Dalbeattie centre is the granite surface of much of the trails, hence the name Hardrock Trail for the 27km red-graded circuit.

This is an extremely popular trail, though Dalbeattie also boasts green (the 10.5km Ironhash) and blue (the 14km Moyle Hill) options. On the Hardrock Trail there are also black-graded features,

including Volunteer Ridge, the Qualifier, the Terrible Twins, and of course The Slab, but there are 'chicken runs' and alternatives for those who don't fancy them.

The Hardrock Trail begins with a lengthy fireroad climb before Moyle Magic, the first and very pleasant bit of singletrack. It is fairly technical from the start, with some climbing and fiddly bits, and, not far from the start, a very deep, fast bombhole.

After braving or bypassing The Slab (the alternative being via a superb stretch of singletrack), the route undulates through open forest with expansive views and then on to trails that are by turns rocky, rooty and smooth, downhill, uphill and twisty: an endless variety.

On the approach to the high point of Barcloy Hill, the technical challenges are unrelenting with numerous rocks and large stones to negotiate, requiring good balance and bike handling in places, and views across the Solway Firth. Next come the Terrible Twins – miniature versions of The Slab – though these are also optional.

Spooky Wood II takes you into deep, dark forest – not typical of Dalbeattie – before reaching Jacob's Ladder, another technical challenge, described as 'steep and pitchin''

which gives a fast but short-lived descent down a series of step-like rocks and stones.

More of the same next on Rock Don't Roll, but this time over level ground: this is like a much smaller version of the famous McMoab at Kirroughtree, with rocks and boulders arranged side-by-side.

Although you can find yourself spending a lot of the day riding on fireroads at Dalbeattie, this is a large and open centre with great views of the area and there are enough technical challenges to keep you coming back for more.

Mabie Phoenix Trail

Distance **17km waymarked (Red)**
Map **OS Explorer 313** Facilities **Car park
(fee), bike shop/hire/café, toilets, bike
wash, hotel bar nearby**

**Its infamous Dark Side gives it a
reputation for the extreme, but the mix
of natural and man-made trails in this
small Dumfriesshire forest makes Mabie
a well-balanced and varied experience.**

Mabie forest contains a good mix of trails
but what distinguishes this among the
7Stanes centres is its emphasis on natural
singletrack. Instead of being cut out of the
ground, or covered in imported stones or
granite, many of the trails at Mabie appear to
have been created simply by people riding
there, taking the best or most interesting
lines through the trees, negotiating roots and
other natural obstacles along the way.

It is not all like that and there are some
great man-made trails too, but there seem
to be more roots than rocks at Mabie. The

popular ride here is the red-grade 7km
Phoenix Trail, which begins with singletrack
almost immediately, leaving the footpath
just metres from the trail head to take a
sharp left into the trees. There is only
very limited use of forest roads from here
on in, with the majority of the ride on
glorious singletrack.

The opening Butterhole Climb is a short
but tough and reasonably technical ascent,
with The Ridge, which comes next, more of
a slog over natural ground. But the descents
that follow are fantastic, flowing nicely with
big sweeping berms as well as a couple of
tricky off-camber corners, on a harder,
grippier and more rocky track that
eventually takes you back into the forest.

More singletrack follows, with Contour
Climb and the up-and-down Descender
Bender. A small river crossing, Burn Splash,
leads on to Scorpion, a real leg-burner of a
climb whose name is self-evident. The
ascent is not too long but so steep and

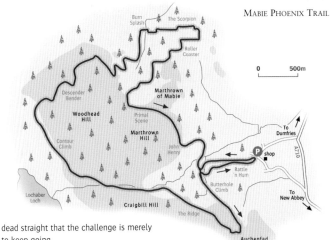

dead straight that the challenge is merely to keep going.

After the classic, fast singletrack of Roller Coaster it's back on to the softer, more rooty ground that Mabie is famous for, as the trail weaves on through this relatively compact forest. Primal Scene, billed as 'higher than the sun sweet singletrack', includes sections of North Shore as it climbs up to a ridge that gives great views across to Dumfries.

Towards the end of the ride there are one or two technical features, such as a balance beam, for those who fancy, before you're on the final section, Rattle 'n' Hum, which drops you back through the forest on a woody, rooty section that offers a satisfying conclusion to the well-balanced and nicely varied Phoenix Trail.

Mabie is also renowned for the Dark Side, which is described as 'the most technically demanding, hair-raising 2km of legal timber trail to be found on Forestry Commission land in this country'.

If the Phoenix Trail is a good cross-country ride that is suitable for a wide range of abilities (there are also the 8.2km green-graded Big Views loop and blue-graded 11.2km Woodhead plus 19km Lochbank Loops, which use mainly wider paths), then the Dark Side is at the other extreme.

Extreme is the word: it makes Ewok Village at Glentress seem like bumping off the kerb. Situated in a corner of the forest, away from the main trails, the Dark Side is a notoriously difficult section of North Shore trails, which are also referred to as 'north sore' by the riders who have fallen while attempting to negotiate trails as narrow as 10cm and up to 1m high, rising to double that in the case of the gap jump.

The Dark Side is strictly for experts only, hence the double diamond black grading. Even then, those who do want to try it are advised to walk the Dark Side first.

The Ae Line

Distance **24km waymarked (Red)**
Map **OS Explorer 321** Facilities **Shop in Ae
Village, uplift service**

**Its focus on thrills and fun with big
jumps, berms and drop-offs makes Ae
a sublime experience.**

The man-made trails in the Forest of Ae
are different in character to this area's other
7Stanes centres at Mabie, Dalbeattie and
Kirroughtree. The trails are cut directly
out of the earth, with any stone that's
added coming from the forest itself,
meaning that they do not have the softer
and more natural feel of Mabie, the
hard granite of Dalbeattie or the black
shale of Kirroughtree.

The forest, which sits on the shoulder
dividing Nithsdale from Annandale, has
long been a popular spot for mountain
biking, but mainly for downhillers, with
well-established tracks drawing riders
here in large numbers for both practice
and racing.

But a red-graded trail, the Ae Line, was
added in 2005 and it has proved a real hit.
It does seem to owe something to the
influence of the downhill side of the sport
in terms of design and construction. There
is a big emphasis on thrills and fun, with
numerous jumps, drop-offs and tabletops,
particularly in a final section of singletrack
downhill that lays these features on thick
and fast, providing a full-on – and, in one

or two places, airborne – descent back to the car park.

The Ae-Line is 24km, with blue and green trails being developed. The opening section of singletrack, which is well-signposted and accessed from a corner of the car park, is known as Rab's Slippy One. It is a sublime uphill stretch that winds through the trees

on a well-made track that is often coated in a soft, luxuriant cover of pine needles.

This is all very pleasant to ride on, but not altogether typical of the trails at Ae. Those that come later are harder packed, they swoop and soar and tend to be of the rollercoaster variety, with huge tabletops, jumps and berms.

There is quite a bit of ascent, too, in the form of meandering, zigzagging climbs on singletrack or on stretches of fireroad, with some of the singletrack – Granny Green Luv, Bran Burn Bash – covering high and very exposed ground.

The Edge signals an end to the climbing, and it is, as it sounds, a thin strip of singletrack that follows a high ridge with a steep drop on one side to the river. Coming off the ridge, the trail then ducks into the dark forest, twisting through the trees and losing a lot of height in a relatively short distance via a series of fast bermed corners.

Nil Desperandum and the Omega Man are the final sections of singletrack, both of them long, spectacular and thrilling to ride, with big bermed corners, tabletops, jumps, doubles and drop-offs. Right at the end there are even optional beam bars and other obstacles for trials-type manoeuvres.

For those who fancy the downhill track, this is 1.6km long and includes the infamous 6.7m Coffin Jump, which at least is a lot less cryptic than the names given to sections of the Ae Line.

Newcastleton Red

Distance **13km waymarked (Red with 0.5km Black section)** Maps **OS Explorer 324 and Explorer OL 42** Facilities **Toilets on site, pub, shop in Newcastleton**

Known for its family-friendly trails, this buzzing 7Stanes centre also has a nice red route with optional black section.

Newcastleton is the smallest of the 7Stanes centres, but it is home to some great trails and a thriving local mountain biking scene. In particular it's billed as a good venue for families and novices, but don't let this create the impression that it has nothing for the more experienced mountain biker.

Indeed, its reputation as the family-friendly centre in the 7Stanes stable seems a little unfair. There is more to Newcastleton than the very straightforward blue routes (there are two), or the 0.4km green skills loop, which is certainly ideal for young mountain bikers or beginners.

Its centrepiece is a 13km red route with a testing 0.5km black ridge section near the beginning. Perhaps not an epic day out, but they are nice trails to ride all the same. And with Kielder Forest just across the border, there is always the potential to seek out longer routes.

The singletrack, though, is enough to begin with. From the car park, a steep but

short-lived climb takes you through a gate and almost straight on to singletrack where the blue, red or black options all plunge down into the forest. The skills loop, with tabletops and bombholes, also starts here.

These trails are well built, with some interesting features. Right at the beginning, there is the option of the Black Ridge, which takes a direct line of descent while the red route slaloms down through the forest via a succession of switchbacks.

The Black Ridge comprises some technical North Shore, drop-offs and balance beams, and requires steady bike handling and keen balance. The red route is less technical, but it's fast, swoopy and great fun as it snakes up and down the hill before heading into the Hidden Valley.

At first, the second stretch of singletrack can be boggy and slippy, with large and exposed roots to negotiate, followed by big tree trunks that have been laid side by side to give a bumpy crossing over more soggy terrain.

Next comes a long uphill slog on fireroad, intersecting with the blue trails and the Cross Border Trail that links Newcastleton with Kielder Forest. There are plans to develop more mountain bike options around this, since Kielder, which is England's largest forest, has always been a popular location for mountain biking.

Back into the trees and you're on to more singletrack for a boulder crossing which is treacherous when wet, before a river crossing, which can be avoided via an arched bridge. Some timber trails follow over a section known, unsurprisingly, as The Bog, leading to a steep uphill section of singletrack.

After another stretch of forest road, it's on to another singletrack climb, this time to reach the moonscape of Dead Man's Quarry, before Swarf Hill, on the Swarf Quarry trail. A final welcome descent takes you back to the start.

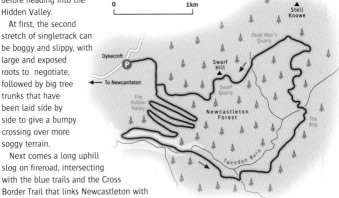

33

There is a huge range of mountain biking experiences to be had throughout Central Scotland, including, perhaps surprisingly, some hidden gems.

The Pentlands, on the outskirts of Edinburgh, could never be described as such. The vast network of paths and trails that zigzag across these hills have provided an introduction to mountain biking for many thousands of people, not least because they are so close to the capital.

But less familiar, and almost as accessible, is the Fife Coastal Path. This is a long-distance trail that follows a fantastic stretch of coastline, popular with walkers but – as yet – virtually unknown to mountain bikers.

This section also features the island of Arran, which has always been a brilliant destination for outdoors enthusiasts and can now boast a growing network of mountain biking trails.

The only dedicated mountain biking centre featured here is Carron Valley, a forest that's handily placed between Glasgow and Stirling, where excellent singletrack trails have been designed and built by local mountain bikers.

There are some great rides on the outskirts of Glasgow, which include parts of Scotland's most popular long-distance trail, the West Highland Way, and an urban escape to Gleniffer Braes.

Finally, there's a lung-busting climb to the summit of Dumyat, near Stirling, followed by an exhilarating descent.

Central Scotland

A Pentland Adventure

Distance **22km unmarked**
Map **OS Explorer 344**
Facilities **Pub at Carlops**

The Pentland hills, to the south of Edinburgh, give a stunning backdrop to this fair weather route with technical climbing and smooth downhills.

This is a classic Pentlands circuit, lying just far enough away from Edinburgh to allow you to climb over the hills and into an area that can feel about as far removed from the city as some of the most remote parts of the Highlands. Remarkably, the city is barely 24km away.

The tracks here are popular among walkers and runners and ideal for mountain bikers, though some are sensitive to erosion and care should be taken on certain paths. Some of these are signposted accordingly, warning that bikes are unsuitable.

From the south end of Carlops village follow a landrover track that climbs up to North Esk Reservoir. It is here that the path narrows and it is a nice singletrack trail that curls around the far end of the small reservoir, before heading up the glen between Cock Rig and Wether Law in the direction of Balerno.

What follows is best described as a 'technical climb'. Not everyone's cup of tea, perhaps, because it's a long slog that's boggy and rutted in places. The path traverses the side of Cock Rig, meaning there's an awkward camber in places, and it requires a serious effort to keep the momentum going. But the bonus is that it carries you into a stunning landscape of rolling hills that feels seriously remote, without a road in sight.

Over the top of the hill past Bore Stane and there is some good, gradual downhill over wider, more established tracks – with large sections covered by wooden platforms, or tree trunks lying side by side, over ground that gets very boggy. This can be seriously slippy when wet.

Though there are no roads, there are lots of signposts. Here, you are following the signs to Bavelaw. At the end of the track, near Listonshiels, the trail turns right to cut across the hillside and soon joins a singletrack road. After East Rigg farm comes a T-junction where you will turn right, cross a bridge and face a monstrous climb up through a steep avenue of trees.

At the top, turn right and then immediately left, through the gate and on to a path that is signposted Nine Mile Burn. There's more serious climbing here, first up Hare Hill, which is just as hard going as Cock Rig but on better tracks. Heading in the direction of West Kip, you then turn up Cap Law.

At the top there is one track heading straight on to Penicuik, or another heading over Monk's Rig, but the latter is not recommended for riding in winter or when it's wet, since sections of it are vulnerable to erosion.

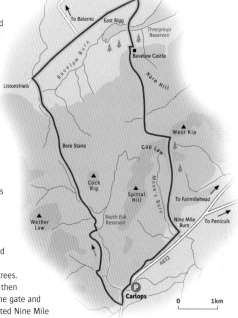

Taking the track in the direction of Penicuik drops you on to the main A702 road, leaving an 8km journey back to Carlops. Alternatively, in dry conditions the ride over Monk's Rig, which includes a fantastic descent on a soft, grassy surface, brings you out at Nine Mile Burn, from where a singletrack road runs parallel to the main road, and ends with a brief singletrack trail back to Carlops.

37

Kingdom of Fife Coastal Path

Distance **130km waymarked**
Maps **OS Landranger 59 and 65**
Facilities **Pubs, shops, cafés en route**

This is an absolute gem of a long-distance trail, with sections of it popular with walkers and virtually all of it perfect for mountain biking – though keep a considerate eye out for those walkers, especially on the later East Neuk section.

For the quality of the trails, and the riding experience they provide, this should be near the top of any mountain biker's 'must do' list for Scotland. It includes spectacular beaches and caves, pretty villages and stunning views across the Forth, as well as – crucially as far as mountain bikers are concerned – fantastic singletrack trails.

At a total distance of 130km, the trail officially starts in Culross, roughly halfway between the Forth and Kincardine bridges.

But a popular starting point is the train station at Inverkeithing, just over the Forth bridges, or Kirkcaldy, further up the coast.

This early chunk is pleasant but mostly on paths as opposed to trails, with Edinburgh and the adjacent port of Leith dominating the view across the Forth. After Burntisland there's a lengthy section using roads and passing an enormous caravan park, before you enter Kinghorn, where the trail drops steeply down on to a delightful little crescent-shaped beach.

Beyond Kinghorn the path becomes a bit wilder, narrower and tighter: there are sections of singletrack here that offer a taste of what's to come, hugging the edges of the many golden beaches.

Along the promenade at Kirkcaldy and then it's back on roads (though roads account for only a small percentage of the total distance covered) between Buckhaven and Leven. It is after Leven that the trail, as it enters the picturesque East Neuk of Fife, becomes truly spectacular.

At the end of the Leven promenade there are low and high tide options: the former being to ride along the sand, though a surface coating of stones makes it quite rideable; with the latter taking you along a good path at the top of the beach.

On to Largo, the first of a series of pretty villages, where the real highlights of this ride begin. Along the coast, you start to negotiate tight, narrow, twisting paths, set back a little from the beach and through long grass, in places hip height. All this makes the path difficult to see, and invisible beyond about a metre ahead of you, but it also makes for great mountain biking, demanding concentration and full commitment. The sensation is similar to downhill riding but at a vastly reduced speed. The price of a misjudgment, therefore, is very low, with grass and sand ensuring a soft landing.

From here, the Fife headland juts out in front of you. This is the East Neuk, with the trail delivering you to the neighbouring villages of Earlsferry and Elie, following one of the only serious climbs of the entire route.

If there is time it is worth stepping off the bike on the cliff section to have a look at the famous Elie Chain Walk — modelled on the via ferrata you find in the Italian Dolomites, where chains are fastened to the rock to help climbers and walkers negotiate the terrain. It's on a much smaller scale but still good fun.

After Elie the path gets even better, with numerous attractions, including ruins, lighthouses, a windmill and open air swimming pool at St Monans, and an incredible rock formation on the beach between Anstruther and Crail.

The further north the path goes, the wilder it gets. By Kingsbarns Golf Links, though, it may be too rough for some. An option here is to avoid the northeast corner of Fife, where the trail becomes more barren and less rideable, and to head by road to Leuchars train station via St Andrews.

Dumyat of the Ochils

Distance **17km unmarked**
Map **OS Explorer 366** Facilities **Bike shop, pubs, shops, cafés, toilets in Bridge of Allan**

A 'proper' climb up and down Dumyat provides an energy-sapping ascent from Stirling University and an exhilarating return to Bridge of Allan. With big climbs and some severe drops close to the path, this route is best for fit, competent bike handlers.

The summits of real mountains are seldom actually negotiable by bike. Just occasionally, though, you get to tackle a hill that proves that 'mountain bike' isn't a misnomer – and Dumyat, near Stirling, is one such lump of rock.

In its imposing position at the western end of the Ochils, 418m above sea level,

Dumyat is a striking hill and very popular among both walkers and mountain bikers. The fact that it juts out of the plains around Stirling and the source of the Forth only adds to the impression at its summit that you are a lot higher than you actually are.

The ride to that point is challenging, naturally. It involves a long, relentless climb that takes you up to very exposed hillside, but most is rideable: there are only two or three sections where you may want to dismount. That said, at certain times it can be boggy in places, making the ride more difficult, especially in winter.

Our ride begins in Bridge of Allan, taking in some fast and winding trails along the west bank of the beautiful Allan Water for 1.5km before crossing the river and heading up the lower slopes of Dumyat itself.

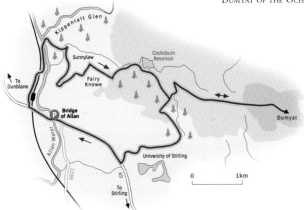

After passing Cocksburn Reservoir the trail takes you out to the Sheriffmuir road and on to Dumyat, where a punishing climb now begins.

Over the stile, and it's best to follow the higher of the upward-trending paths. At the bottom, it tends to be wide but steep in places. Later, as the path thins out, it becomes more rocky and, in places, very narrow indeed, including fairly precarious sections where it clings tightly to the side of the hill, with serious drop-offs on one side. Towards the top there are a couple of sections where, if you were to fall, you wouldn't want it to be to the right.

As the path continues you find yourself considerably higher than the Wallace Monument, the local landmark that is visible for miles. As you rise still higher, there are fantastic panoramic views across the Forth Valley, all the way to Edinburgh and the Pentland Hills.

At the summit of Dumyat there is a beacon and a memorial to the Argyll and Sutherland Highlanders. It is exposed up here and mountain bikers can find the wind one of the challenges towards the summit. The ride down, though, provides ample recompense: retrace the top path, which is tight, steep and rocky, with softer ground as you continue down. It is challenging but not too technical.

And, of course, it is a decent length, giving 4.5km of virtually uninterrupted downhill to reach the campus of Stirling University, followed shortly by Bridge of Allan. As you descend, there are also options off to the left, with paths that lead down in the direction of the Logie Kirk car park (an alternative start point).

Whichever route you take, this is an exhilarating mountain biking experience and suitable for a huge range of abilities, from those who will take all day to riders who will blast up and down in less than a couple of hours.

Carron Valley Kelpie Trails

Distance 9.3km waymarked (Red)
Map OS Explorer 348 Facilities Pubs, shop, café in Fintry, pub at Carronbridge

Fast and flowing with a succession of technical features to add to the fun at the end, Carron Valley is deserving of the reputation that's spreading beyond its Central Scotland base.

The trails at Carron Valley are the result of the sterling efforts of mainly Stirling-based mountain bikers to establish a quality facility in Central Scotland. The Carron Valley Development Group raised significant funding and managed the building of the new trails – known as Carron Valley's Kelpie Trails – which opened to the public in March 2006.

This place has been popular among mountain bikers for years: first, because it is so handy for major population centres, including Glasgow, Stirling and Falkirk; second, because there is an existing network of forest roads and tracks; and third, because the Carron Valley covers such a vast area.

The CVDG hope that the new trails are just the beginning. But they have made a good start: the first trails are well designed and constructed, and suitable for a wide range of abilities.

Graded red by the Forestry Commission, they are in the main flowing and not too technical, but with the sting in the tail of a fun park – an ungraded final section – with features that are as challenging as you want them to be, dependent largely on how fast you ride them.

Starting from the car park, there's the familiar slog up forest road to the first section of singletrack, Pipedream, which here offers little respite, cutting back on the

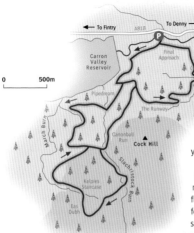

definitely the most challenging feature on the Kelpie Trails.

The trail corkscrews on down through the trees, not steep but with tight corners, some off-camber. But there is nothing too technical here: it meanders downhill and spits you back out on the forest road.

Then it's briefly up again, to join the exhilarating, and hence appropriately named, Cannonball Run – a fast, flowing section of trail that introduces features such as jumps, doubles, and a spectacularly large and deep bermed corner at the end.

forest road before winding uphill. This trail offers good views down over the Carron Valley Reservoir, and across to Meikle Bin.

Then it's back on forest roads, and up to the highest point of the circuit and the start of a downhill section of around 1.5km known as Eas Dubh – Gaelic for 'black water', in recognition of the four waterfalls that the trail passes.

This descent is not steep, but it includes a couple of abrupt, rocky drops, with the Kelpies' Staircase, in particular, a forbidding obstacle when viewed from the top. Its negotiation is made a little more straightforward, however, by a broad 'landing pad' at the bottom of the 0.6m-wide rock-strewn drop, allowing plenty of room for manoeuvre. That said, this is

The character of the trails change as you ride round, becoming progressively faster, and inevitably a little more adrenaline-charged. Or perhaps this is simply a consequence of tired legs. But the final section, known as The Runway on account of it lying directly under the flightpath to Glasgow Airport, is well deserving of its description as a fun park area.

At around 1.5km long, The Runway comprises a dizzying succession of berms, tabletops and doubles, all of them coming thick and fast, until Final Approach finishes the ride.

Unless – and this will doubtless prove a popular option for many – you want another go at some of those doubles, in which case it's an easy ride back up the forest road to tackle The Runway again.

Mugdock and the Campsies

Distance **26km unmarked**
Map **OS Landranger 64 or Explorer 348**
Facilities **Pubs, shops, cafés in Milngavie**

Follow the West Highland Way from its start into Mugdock Country Park and beyond to the Campsie Fells on a rugged ride with stunning views.

This is a route that takes you out of the suburbs of the vast, sprawling city of Glasgow and into countryside that could almost belong to the remote, rugged Highlands. For that reason alone it is both easy to access and ride, and quite spectacular in places.

Starting from Milngavie, an attractive suburb, the direct route out of town is along the West Highland Way, Scotland's best known long-distance footpath, which starts at the north end of the railway station. Some 152km long in total, it stretches all the way up to Fort William by way of drove roads, and old military and coaching roads, via Loch Lomond, with stretches of it good for mountain biking.

While once cycling tended to be discouraged, mountain biking on the West Highland Way has become more popular, even if in parts it isn't particularly rideable. But the early section heading out of Milngavie and towards the Campsie Fells is just about perfect.

It climbs gradually from the town centre, along an old railway line and then by the banks of the Allander Water. Over Drumclog Moor it becomes more rugged before entering Mugdock Country Park, where there are numerous opportunities to leave the

Way and explore some of the singletrack: the place is riddled with little trails, many of them very popular among local mountain bikers.

On leaving the park and its woodland, everything opens up with views of the Campsie Fells and even, on a clear day, Ben Lomond. The track here is occasionally lumpy and rocky as it passes Craigallian Loch and makes its gradual climbs past the Carbeth huts, before the West Highland Way takes you across a minor road and over a stile to re-join the path. It is well signposted.

The next stretch of the Way, leading to Glengoyne distillery, provides excellent mountain biking terrain: a narrow path, with loose stones, rises and plummets back down, and gives good views of Dumgoyne, the distinctive peak on the western edge of the Campsies.

Sitting beneath it is the distinctive bleached white building of Glengoyne distillery. As it draws nearer, you leave the West Highland Way, joining the road for a few hundred metres before heading round the back of the distillery and taking a rough track that climbs steeply via several hairpins towards a gate.

Beyond the gate a waterboard track – sturdy and rideable in all weather – traverses the hill, undulating without any significant climbs or descents. Here you are riding alongside the pipes that reach all the way from Loch Katrine to Glasgow's reservoirs to provide water for the city.

The track comes out eventually at Blanefield, where you join the main road through the village. A right and then a quick left turn drop you on to a small path heading out of Blanefield in the direction of Mugdock Country Park, by way of a couple of residential areas and two stiff climbs on narrow paths.

There are several routes back through the park, one of them taking you round by the castle and Mugdock Loch before you re-join the West Highland Way for the final 2km back to Milngavie town centre.

Gleniffer Braes Escape

Distance **8km unmarked**
Map **OS Landranger 64**
Facilities **Pubs, shops, café in Barrhead**

Escape from Glasgow on a labyrinth of tracks deep in this country park, with some superb off-camber singletrack and a steep flight of steps to give added excitement at the end.

Glasgow, the 'dear green place', has more parks than most cities. And although the hill and parkland known as Gleniffer Braes doesn't fall within the city boundaries, being about 5km south of Paisley, it is within easy reach of Glasgow, and the views across the city are stunning.

It's hard to believe the proximity of this place to such a major urban – and industrial – centre, nor that it is possible to ride for several hours, into deepest Renfrewshire, with only a couple of road crossings likely to provide close-up

sightings of cars. Otherwise, Gleniffer, like the Pentlands on the outskirts of Edinburgh, offers an instant escape from the city, as well as a fantastic contrast.

There is a labyrinthine network of routes. Tracks and paths criss-cross the hill and parkland, so there are endless options and loads of routes to link up. There is a good mix of path types, too, with wider trails and thin strips of singletrack.

A decent loop, around 8km in length, can be accessed from Caplathill Road (also known locally as the Paisley road). From Brownside Farm, on the outskirts of Barrhead, a track climbs up the hill: it's a bit of a slog but you quickly gain enough height to enjoy the first of those views across the relatively flat urban landscape spread out before you. It stretches for miles, and in most directions.

On the ascent are several gates, one marking the entrance to Gleniffer Braes

Country Park, with a map detailing the Fereneze Brae paths network, which can help plot a mountain biking route, or, indeed, several. From here the path climbs the hill in steep hairpin bends before levelling out and undulating along one of the higher points, in the direction of Glenburn Reservoir. A gate leads into a field, populated by inquisitive Highland cattle, thus providing another slightly surreal juxtaposition with the city below.

Through the gate and a sharp left takes you up a rough, rutted path on a technical climb that isn't always rideable all the way up: it can be a bit muddy in places. But at the top the surface improves and you pick up signposts for the Fereneze paths network. To the right is Glenburn Reservoir, to the left is Killoch Glen via Harelaw Reservoir, which is the direction to head in.

This takes you to the edge of a golf course, but just before hitting the manicured fairways a path darts off to the right, and you follow that for about 200m before taking another right, signposted Killoch Glen and Paisley via Glenburn Reservoir. The paths around here are narrower, slightly rougher and use boardwalk in places to carry you and bike over boggy ground. There is some good off-camber singletrack on the way back

down to Gateside, and from here it's a 10-minute ride on the road back to the starting point.

The real challenge, towards the end, is a section of steps – 65 in all, and steep, with a sharp right-hander at the bottom. Not recommended other than for the most skilled bike handlers, because braking isn't an option on the way down – and there are no escape routes.

Generally, though it's 'escape' that sums up Gleniffer Braes – it's a great, easy break from the city, and it offers all manner of paths, tracks and terrain to have a bit of fun and ride for just about any length of time, from 30 minutes to several hours.

Goat Tracks on Arran

Distance **18km waymarked (Red)**
Map **OS Explorer 361** Facilities **Bike shop/hire in Brodick, pubs, shops, cafés in Brodick and Lamlash**

Arran's red and black trails take you largely off-road onto some fantastic, gnarly, testing singletrack around Brodick and Lamlash.

There's a lot happening on the island of Arran, with new mountain biking trails being established and waymarked. And of course the island, which is often dubbed Scotland in Miniature, also boasts the mountains, deep glens, burns and beaches that make for perfect mountain biking terrain, whichever direction you turn.

The first waymarked trail on Arran was a blue-graded route based around Brodick Castle. Aimed principally at entry level mountain bikers, it contains a fair amount of climbing – we should warn that all the trails on Arran do – making it a good introduction for the less experienced rather than a challenging outing for the more adventurous riders.

For them, there are red and black trails now established too, both waymarked and offering exceptional mountain biking. Both start in the village of Brodick and explore the south of the island. Most appealing is the fact that both routes also take you through the village of Lamlash, which at one time competed with Brodick as the main ferry port on the island. There are shops and usually lots going on here, especially during the tourist season.

The red route, which is a figure-of-eight

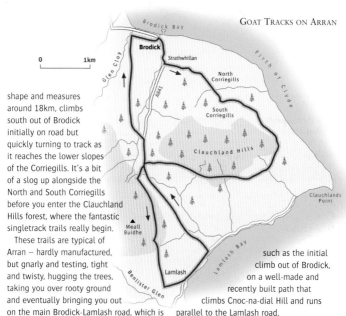

shape and measures around 18km, climbs south out of Brodick initially on road but quickly turning to track as it reaches the lower slopes of the Corriegills. It's a bit of a slog up alongside the North and South Corriegills before you enter the Clauchland Hills forest, where the fantastic singletrack trails really begin.

These trails are typical of Arran – hardly manufactured, but gnarly and testing, tight and twisty, hugging the trees, taking you over rooty ground and eventually bringing you out on the main Brodick-Lamlash road, which is the intersection of the figure-of-eight loop.

After crossing this road and re-joining the trail there's a good, fast descent into Lamlash. Then you ride through the village – the only section of road, really, on the entire route – before joining a new trail that runs parallel to the Lamlash-Brodick road. Not that you'd know it – as the singletrack ducks into the forest, the road becomes invisible. The route finishes with another good descent, on a flowing, well-made bit of singletrack, into Brodick.

The black route is more of an epic, being 25km in length but with an optional loop to extend it to 32km – a hard day out. It shares some of the red route's trails, in some cases going in the other direction,

such as the initial climb out of Brodick, on a well-made and recently built path that climbs Cnoc-na-dial Hill and runs parallel to the Lamlash road.

Dropping into Lamlash it then heads north to Glen Kilm farm, climbing on good forest roads through Dyemill to above Whiting Bay before returning via superb singletrack to Dyemill. Back to Lamlash and the intersection of the figure-of-eight red route on the Brodick-Lamlash road, and then there's the option of the extra 7km loop. This takes you into the natural trails of Clauchlands forest and finishes eventually with a descent down into Glen Cloy.

A new 10km blue-graded route also exists, again using some of the same trails, sharing the black climb out of Brodick (which is also the final descent on the red route), before heading straight down into Glen Cloy and returning to Brodick.

49

In terms of the sheer diversity of its mountain biking, Scotland's North-east has got it all: centres with man-made singletrack trails, stunning natural paths and tracks and epic all-day or multi-day expeditions.

Kirkhill, the forest on the outskirts of Aberdeen that sits on Tyrebagger Hill, is a mecca for mountain bikers from the surrounding area. As well as a fun park section of singletrack, it includes trails and loops that attract both experienced bikers and those new to the sport.

For the ultimate singletrack experience in the North-east, though, Laggan is the place to go. The Wolftrax promises mountain biking with bite, and this centre, with café and bike shop, is an enormously popular fixture on Scotland's mountain biking scene.

Further north, in Moray, there is more quality singletrack, thanks to the ambitious development of the Moray Monster Trails. Around 30km of singletrack has been built to link up three distinct centres, at Ordiequish, Whiteash and Ben Aigan.

In the North-east of Scotland there is also an epic mountain ride, to the summit of Mount Keen, and a collection of smaller hills, just outside Aberdeen, which can be explored very easily from the city.

This section also includes the Cairngorms, Britain's largest national park which, many claim, contains the best mountain biking in the country. There are numerous options here, and throughout the Spey Valley as well, from small spins in Rothiemurchus Estate to big rides deep into the heart of the Cairngorm mountains.

North-east Scotland

Elgin

INVERNESS

Keith

7

6 Grantown-on-Spey

Aviemore

Inverurie **9**
10

Kingussie **5**
4
3
ABERDEEN

Laggan
2

Aboyne
8

Dunkeld **1**

PERTH

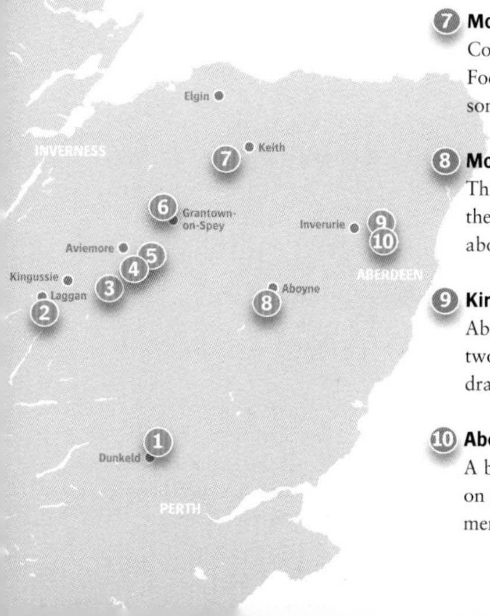

The Queen's Road from Dunkeld

Distance **45km unmarked**
Map **OS Landranger 53**
Facilities **Pubs, shops, cafés in Dunkeld**

This is a great summertime touring route for those wanting to test their endurance in some truly wild country.

Dunkeld stands on the edge of some of the most dramatic and remote Perthshire countryside, and it forms a gateway to excellent mountain biking. On the south side of this picturesque cathedral town, 20km north of Perth, are the woods around the Hermitage, with a network of forest tracks which are good for mountain biking but also very popular with walkers. Here, too, there are several downhill mountain biking tracks, and Dunkeld is a popular venue for downhill racing.

But to the north of the town is the area known as Cally and Loch Ordie, a vast wilderness that offers a multitude of mountain biking options, from short rides around Loch Ordie to epic days out or even multi-day rides, all the way to Pitlochry or along the old Queen's Road to Braemar.

The Queen in question here is Victoria, and this 'road' – a loose description for a track that is rough today and wouldn't have been much smoother in the 19th century, when negotiated in a horse and carriage – was the most direct route between Perth and Braemar. It still is, but only walkers and mountain bikers are likely to tackle it. A section of it has also been 'lost' – and a mountain bike is perhaps not the best mode of transport for anyone who wants to find it.

There is a fantastic ride, in any case,

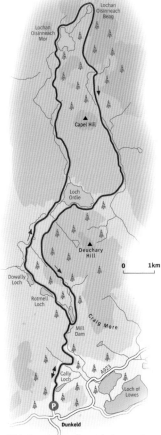

Through a gate and after about 200m there's a sharp right on to a narrower trail, though it's a little wider than singletrack: single-and-a-half track might be more accurate. What follows is a long, technical climb, which is steep at times. It is also rocky and rutted in places, with channels permanently filled with running water.

Nearing the summit and the wilderness unfolds before you: to the left is the distinctive profile of Schiehallion, one of many peaks that can be seen in a panorama that extends for miles in all directions.

The path now takes you downhill to Mill Dam along its shoreline before climbing again up to Loch Ordie. This remains good and perfectly rideable until just after the loch, when it becomes more rugged and covered in places by scraggy heather. There is more climbing after Loch Ordie, at the end of which you go through a gate and bear right, up to Sarah's Bothy, the highest point of the ride.

Skirt the edge of Lochan Oisinneach Mor and Lochan Oisinneach Beag, before the long descent back to Mill Dam. It's not super fast or particularly technical, but this downhill stretch flows nicely and comes as a decent reward after so much climbing.

This is a route that fit riders can do in a day: it's an endurance touring ride rather than one for those seeking the adrenaline rush of highly technical singletrack.

The only note of caution would be that it's best avoided in winter, when, given the height, snow and ice is more than likely for at least two-thirds of the total distance.

which doesn't go as far as the lost section of the old Queen's Road. From the Cally car park, situated 400m into the forest, follow the forest road as it climbs steadily in the direction of Mill Dam (you can also start from Dunkeld train station).

Laggan Wolftrax

Distance 8.9km waymarked (Red with Blue sections) **Map** OS Explorer 400 **Facilities** Bike shop/hire, café, toilets, showers, bike wash

'With bite' is an apt description for Laggan with its gloriously narrow singletrack, elevated North Shore and big air possibilities. And that's before you even start talking about the black trail.

Laggan could stake a claim for being the best all-round mountain biking centre in Scotland. It is on a smaller scale than Glentress, yet it can boast a mountain bikers' café, bike shop and Wolftrax trails (named after the infamous Wolf of Badenoch) that include something for everyone – a claim that is often made, but in this case with real justification.

It is an ambitious set-up: a Glentress for the Highlands. And it is proving a hit, not least because the café and bike shop help to create a welcoming, friendly atmosphere for mountain bikers, as well as back-up and service in the case of emergency.

There are blue-, red- and black-graded trails, each one catering for different tastes and levels of ability. Blue is brief but perfect for those who are new to the sport; the longer red is a classic cross-country experience; and black – well, the black trails at Laggan are beyond what exists at most other centres. They really have to be seen to be believed.

From the car park the outward route is the same for all three routes: a forest road that zigzags up through the trees, bringing you out at the entrance to the blue fun park. In total, the blue ride is 2.3km – a blast down a trail of solid singletrack that

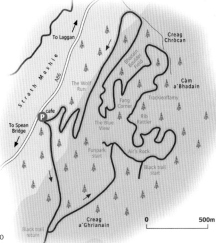

includes big berms, tabletops and gap jumps (doubles). It is suitable for beginners, who can roll over these features, or for more experienced mountain bikers, who will relish the big air possibilities of tackling the fun park at speed.

Continue past the fun park entrance, though, for the red or black routes. The entrance to the 7.8km black route comes first. It's actually graded double diamond black, which hints at its true severity. It is a very technical, tight trail with no chicken runs. It is recommended only for expert mountain bikers, with dual suspension bikes and elbow and knee protection also advised.

Among the challenges are the enormous drop-off known as Two-ton Drop, a boulderfield known as Stiletto Staircase and serious rock slabs that come in such quick succession that you don't even have time to smirk at the names – the Back Attack, the Crack Attack and the Sack Attack.

The black option will prove beyond a lot of mountain bikers, so it's just as well that the red is a more manageable prospect. This trail has won a whole army of admirers. The entrance is a little further up the fireroad, and it features gloriously narrow singletrack that curls around the top of the hill.

There are challenging little features – such as the black-graded Air's Rock – but also chicken runs around the more technical bits. Among the highlights are rock causeways such as Rib Rattler and another rock feature, the Bhadain Boulder Field. There is also a long stretch of elevated North Shore trail – the 240m long Wolf Run – that enters the forest and twists around the trees. It's an exhilarating section that spits you out just above the blue fun park, which you join for the final blast down to the car park.

For many, the red route at Laggan represents the very best of man-made mountain biking trails: narrow, well-made paths that twist and turn, climbing and dropping and meandering to provide an endlessly stimulating and pleasurable ride. It will have you wishing the trails were just that bit longer.

Glen Feshie Challenge

Distance **22km unmarked**
Maps **OS Landranger 35 and 36**
Facilities **Pub, shop in Kincraig**

This is a tough, technical ride for Cairngorms aficionados, designed to test even the most committed rider's fitness, skill and endurance.

Situated in the massively picturesque Glen Feshie, this route may be deceiving in its short length – but don't be fooled. It is basically a climb up to Munro height, a jaunt round the tops of the westernmost Cairngorms, then a steep and rocky drop back down into the glen.

And it will thus test all your mountain biking skills in one go: you have to be fit to complete the climb with any kind of

dignity; you have to show endurance to hack over the tops; and then you have to have some fairly sharp descending and technical skills to complete the descent without tearing holes in your clothes.

Glen Feshie is a superb area for mountain biking in the Cairngorms. There are a number of trails leading up the glen, and some excellent trails linking in with the rest of the Cairngorms network. It can be a base for a week-long trip, riding out into other areas from this central point, or a link for expedition length rides to pass through from south to north, breaching the Cairngorms bulk with some truly amazing singletrack.

A good starting point for this ride is the car park near the end of the singletrack road into the glen, 1km north of Auchlean. Ride south along the road for a short distance, then follow the trails down the east bank of the River Feshie to the footbridge about 800m beyond Auchlean, where you can cross and continue up the

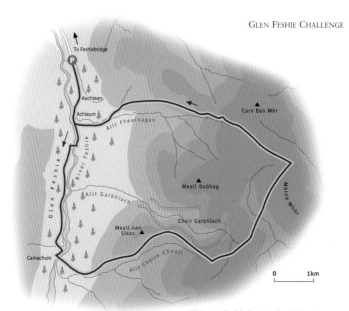

road or keep going via the challenging singletrack on the east bank.

At Carnachuin, turn left and begin the long slog of a climb eastwards up the flanks of Meall nan Sleac. The track is all rideable, but keep your speed in check to conserve energy: it goes on for an awfully long time.

Once at the high point of the first climb, take the left fork and undulate your way over the tops toward Mòine Mhòr. Just as you start to descend from Mòine Mhòr, there is a singletrack trail heading northwest over the moorland by the summit of Carn Bàn Mòr. If you feel like bagging a Munro, take a small detour north to reach this peak, then begin the singletrack descent back into Glen Feshie.

This is rideable but can be tricky in places, with rocks poking out of the peat trail which can alternate between muddy and stony in places. It is superb, but all too soon it drops you out through a band of forest and back to Achleum and the glen floor. Just take your time and don't be too quick to write off reversing the route to climb up the ridge by this section if you want to mix it up a bit, since the added technical difficulties take your mind off the massive height gain you are achieving.

This is a popular ride for Cairngorms mountain biking aficionados, though some do choose to reverse it, climbing via the singletrack and descending the track. Either way, it is a real Highland treat.

Rothiemurchus Lochs Loop

Distance **25km unmarked**
Map **OS Landranger 36** Facilities **Bike
shop/hire, shop, café, toilets in Inverdruie**

**Rothiemurchus is a mountain biking
paradise with a varied network of
natural rooty and cultivated trails at the
heart of the Cairngorms. This route
includes some gorgeous singletrack
complete with water splashes.**

It is difficult to know where to start
with the Cairngorms, or indeed where to
finish. Slap bang in the middle of Britain's
biggest national park, the area includes
the country's largest arctic mountain
landscape and, with its array of paths,
tracks and trails, it is, needless to say,
a mountain biking mecca.

There is huge variety, too. From the
soft paths in the pine forest of the
Rothiemurchus Estate to the tracks that run
through the glens of Feshie and Builg, there
are cultivated tracks and a whole host of
natural trails, many of them rugged and
hard wearing, with the Cairngorm granite
providing the most solid of foundations.

For a 25km ride around Loch an Eilein –
meaning 'loch of the island' in Gaelic – and
then on up to the bothy after Loch Gamhna,
a good starting point is Inverdruie, on the
Cairngorm ski access road, near Aviemore.
From there you're straight into
Rothiemurchus Forest, where it's possible to
explore a huge network of low-level paths
through the trees.

Within the Rothiemurchus Estate
mountain biking is approved, though the
area is understandably very popular with
walkers, too, so care should be taken. Many
of the paths and trails are very well
maintained and they are ideal for mountain
biking: indeed, for those new to the sport

there is much to explore within a very short distance of Inverdruie and a map of recommended routes is available from Rothiemurchus Visitor Centre.

It is tempting to come off the main paths and explore some of the trails that dip in and out of them: however, you are asked not to, and for good reason. Venturing off these is likely to cause erosion and disturb wildlife in this ancient woodland.

On to Loch an Eilein, which is a stunning setting, with the remains of a 12th-century castle on the island. Several good paths skirt the west side, many of them providing ample fun for mountain bikers, with roots to be negotiated and narrow trails running off in all directions.

At the end of the loch there's a good track up to Loch Gamhna. From here there's a fantastic natural singletrack trail, all low level but undulating sharply up and down, with the occasional water crossing: it leads after about 2km to the remote bothy.

It's a case then of retracing the tyre tracks to Loch an Eilein, before heading back to Rothiemurchus Forest, crossing the Cairngorm Club footbridge, passing Loch Morlich and joining the road back to Inverdruie. Alternatively, you can cut back into the Rothiemurchus Estate to take one of the paths running parallel to the road.

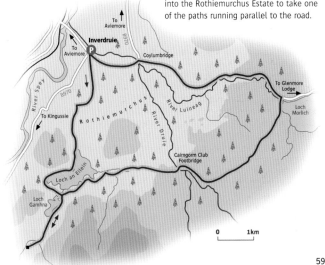

Over the Ryvoan Pass

Distance **28km unmarked**
Map **OS Explorer 403** Facilities **Shop, café, toilets in Glenmore, evening bar at Glenmore Lodge**

A route to challenge the fit rider, this cross-country circuit takes you over two mountain passes with the option of extending your ride on some fun man-made singletrack near the end.

This is a great circular route that uses a popular long-distance path in the Cairngorms before curling around a trio of peaks, joining a remote stretch of singletrack road, and then returning by another famous path.

It is a good cross-country ride, being 28km, but relatively fast thanks to the hard-wearing and weather-resistant tracks. True, there are a couple of leg-bending climbs, but both are perfectly rideable.

There are two possible start points

close to each other, either at Loch Morlich Visitor Centre or by Glenmore Lodge, Scotland's national outdoors centre. Glenmore is closer to the start of the first track: the Ryvoan Pass.

This old drovers' road takes you straight into a quite stunning landscape, through ancient Caledonian pine woodland before the Cairngorm mountain range opens up with the ski area on your right. Riding past An Lochan Uaine you begin to climb steadily but relentlessly on a path that is enjoyable, even allowing for the rocks and stones scattered liberally along its length. Picking your way over and around them keeps things interesting.

The peak that looms large on the left is Meall a'Bhuachaille which is, alas, too steep to tackle on a mountain bike, or else there would be a cracking – not to mention audacious – ride along the ridges of Creagan Gorm and Craiggowrie.

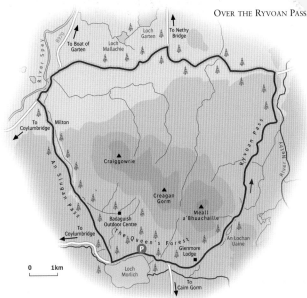

The drovers' road has just the kind of gradient that allows you to keep a decent pace. Climbing up past the Ryvoan bothy – and the start of the path to the summit of Meall a'Bhuachaille – heralds the start of a steep descent, where the main challenge is to pick your way over or around all those loose and occasionally rather large stones and rocks. It has been compared to a dried-up riverbed, which makes for a good, testing stretch of downhill.

The pass forks left before dropping down to a series of forest lodges, where another left turn takes you on to the B970. Follow this quiet road for 1.5km before turning off towards Milton farm and An Slugan Pass – a path that climbs back towards the hills to return you to Glenmore or alternatively to Loch Morlich Visitor Centre.

The early part of An Slugan Pass is steep enough to merit the description leg bender. It's a slog, but the surface is good and riding it shouldn't be a problem for anyone whose fitness isn't too much of an issue.

It rises up into forest, with Craiggowrie, Creagan Gorm and Meall a'Bhuachaille appearing once again on the left shoulder. Over the top, and there is a nice descent into the grounds of the Badaguish Outdoor Centre, where a 10km man-made mountain biking circuit is also very popular.

The singletrack trails at Badaguish, which have hosted numerous races over the years, are well made. They make a good addition to this loop – if you have the energy.

Grantown Singletrack

Distance **15km unmarked**
Map **OS Explorer 419** Facilities **Bike hire, pubs, shops, café, toilets in Grantown**

This ride around Grantown-on-Spey involves tough climbs, great technical singletrack and breathtaking views.

Grantown-on-Spey sits in the Spey Valley, looking across to the Cairngorms, right in the middle of fantastic mountain biking country. There is enormous variety here, from natural singletrack forest trails and big wide tracks across open hillside to disused railways and long-distance paths that are also good in places for mountain biking.

The Speyside Way is one such path, running right through Grantown on its 135km journey between Aviemore and Spey Bay. Some of the path isn't deemed suitable for cycling, including a section of around

12km just north of Grantown, between Cromdale and Ballindalloch, but this can be bypassed by road. Otherwise it is a good, long-distance ride on a decent surface.

From Grantown, though, there is access to great trails. To the east, between the River Spey and the town, is a community-owned forest that contains miles of singletrack trails and forest tracks, much of it suitable for a wide range of abilities.

And at the north end of the town, near the Ian Charles Hospital, the woodland is riddled with more challenging singletrack trails. The best access is from Mossie Road, just 100m from the large car park opposite the Grantown Heritage Museum.

In the trees, a fiddly, technical climb takes you up on to the old railway line which connected Grantown and Forres until the early 1960s.

Following this for about 500m, there is then a trail leading up through the field towards Dreggie Hill. At Wester Dreggie join the singletrack road, entering the Glenbeg estate and linking more wide tracks that skirt Gorton Hill, before climbing up to a remote keeper's cottage.

The views from here take in much of the Spey Valley, towards Cromdale, with the numerous paths and tracks that criss-cross the hills offering a tantalising glimpse of the longer-distance rides that are possible in this area.

Retrace the track back down from the keeper's cottage, turning right at the bottom on to a good off-road trail, from where you can duck into the woods for great, technical singletrack riding. A lot of the tracks here are popular for quad bikes, making them pretty good for mountain biking too.

The path tends to come and go as you drop down the hill, but eventually it leads back to the old railway line, at the old Grantown West station. There are other trails in Beachen Wood, climbing up to the reservoir and past a granite cairn memorial to Paul McLeod, a brilliant skier from Grantown who died, aged 29, in a tragic skiing accident near Chamonix in 2003.

There is a little circuit on harvester tracks that loops around the pools of water known locally as the Black Ponds (which at one time would have held the water for the thirsty steam engines passing through Grantown), before a tricky singletrack descent brings you out once again on the railway line.

63

Moray Monster Trails

Distance **30km (Green, Blue, Red and Black)** Map **OS Explorer 424**
Facilities **Pubs, shops, toilets in Fochabers and Craigellachie**

There's very little that you won't find at the Moray Monster Trails – from natural singletrack to North Shore to family-friendly rides to exposed and technical black trails, all topped off with dazzling views over the Spey Valley.

The Moray Monster trails comprise 30km of singletrack and were designed from the outset to allow mountain bikers to link up the different centres at Fochabers and Ben Aigan. Alternatively, each is a fine venue in its own right.

There are three main access points to the trails, from Ben Aigan, near Craigellachie, or by Ordiequish or Whiteash, which are both at Fochabers.

Starting the ride at Whiteash, the first section of trail is known as The Fochabers Ring, graded red, and 8km in length. From

the car park it starts with flat singletrack that leads to a fireroad and twin track ascent taking you to the Duchess of Richmond Monument.

From there choose either the Fochabers Freeride, with its high North Shore section leading to big earthwork features including jumps, berms and drops, or continue with the Ring, experiencing Mirkwood and other great sections. The Freeride rejoins the Ring and then follows some of the sweetest natural singletrack. Near the end you again have a choice: complete the Ring or cross the A96 to the Wood of Ordiequish.

The Wood of Ordiequish contains no less than five loop trails, from green through blue to black standards, plus a skills area. Again, all the trails are linkable or can be ridden individually. There is a common climb for all the routes. You can choose to ride The Soup Dragon, which is a family-friendly green route and can be extended to include The Dragon's Tail, slightly more challenging but still an easy route.

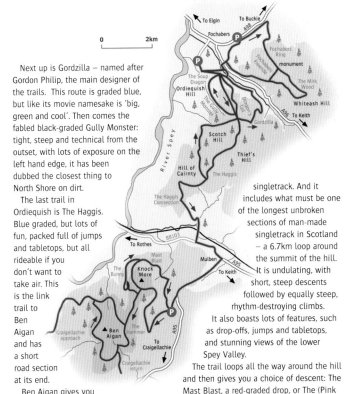

Next up is Gordzilla – named after Gordon Philip, the main designer of the trails. This route is graded blue, but like its movie namesake is 'big, green and cool'. Then comes the fabled black-graded Gully Monster: tight, steep and technical from the outset, with lots of exposure on the left hand edge, it has been dubbed the closest thing to North Shore on dirt.

The last trail in Ordiequish is The Haggis. Blue graded, but lots of fun, packed full of jumps and tabletops, but all rideable if you don't want to take air. This is the link trail to Ben Aigan and has a short road section at its end.

Ben Aigan gives you several trails to choose from. The Ben Aigan Hammer (formerly known as the Summit Trail) comprises the longest route, with the other two trails accessed from here, as is the spur down to the village of Craigellachie. To ride The Hammer followed by either the red or black descents gives a ride of around 15km, most of it on singletrack. And it includes what must be one of the longest unbroken sections of man-made singletrack in Scotland – a 6.7km loop around the summit of the hill. It is undulating, with short, steep descents followed by equally steep, rhythm-destroying climbs. It also boasts lots of features, such as drop-offs, jumps and tabletops, and stunning views of the lower Spey Valley.

The trail loops all the way around the hill and then gives you a choice of descent: The Mast Blast, a red-graded drop, or The (Pink and Fluffy) Bunny, which is well worth its black grading. As well as being steep and fast it's rough and gnarly in places; the Mast, meanwhile, is also fast and packed with jumps. They lead to a section of fireroad that links with a final section of singletrack, taking you, via a series of switchbacks, to the forest car park.

Mount Keen by the Fungle Road

Distance **55km unmarked**
Maps **OS Landranger 44 and 37**
Facilities **Pub, shop, café, toilets in Aboyne**

Starting in Aboyne, this is a long, varied and challenging day out, with early sections ideal for a shorter blast.

The Fungle Road is a route that all Scottish mountain bikers should tackle: it is a classic. And it takes you to Mount Keen, a Munro that climbs to 939m. Of the 284 Munros in Scotland, there are not many that you can ride a bike to the top of, at least not without a lot of frustrating pushing and plodding. Mount Keen, which qualifies for Munro status with a whole 25m to spare, involves only a bit of pushing.

At 55km, this ride is, of course, a very long and tough day out. But it is so varied as to be constantly challenging: from tight woodland singletrack to big, open mountain tracks, it includes pretty much all that's best about Scottish mountain biking.

But for those who don't fancy Munro bagging on a bike, the early part of the Fungle Road is superb for a one- or two-hour blast. The surface is rocky and rooty, with twists and hop-ups to keep it interesting and, in places, quite technical. But that only adds to the fun.

Starting at a large layby near Aboyne, go through the gate and drop down the hill on a dirt track which swings around the south shore of a small lochan just south of Birsemore. This brings you out through a gate onto a track, where you turn left, then left again and climb steadily by Parkside cottage. Join the forest track at the top and stay left. This is now the Fungle Road.

Eventually the Fungle Road takes you

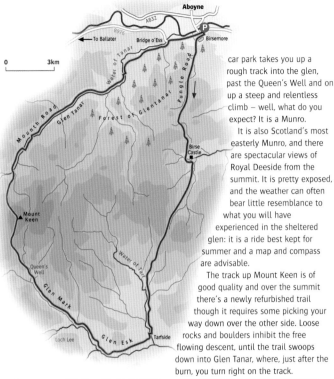

car park takes you up a rough track into the glen, past the Queen's Well and on up a steep and relentless climb – well, what do you expect? It is a Munro.

It is also Scotland's most easterly Munro, and there are spectacular views of Royal Deeside from the summit. It is pretty exposed, and the weather can often bear little resemblance to what you will have experienced in the sheltered glen: it is a ride best kept for summer and a map and compass are advisable.

The track up Mount Keen is of good quality and over the summit there's a newly refurbished trail though it requires some picking your way down over the other side. Loose rocks and boulders inhibit the free flowing descent, until the trail swoops down into Glen Tanar, where, just after the burn, you turn right on the track.

Follow this down to Glen Tanar House, where you're presented with a few options for the descent. Turning right over the bridge, you can follow the track to meet the road at Bridge O'Ess, taking a right here and heading back along the B976, past Birsemore, before the final right turn on to a singletrack road that takes you back to where it all started, in a layby near Aboyne.

onto more open hillside, with estate tracks winding up and over to Birse Castle. Over the pass and the trail peters out for about 500m, necessitating a bit of pushing. Best to shoulder the bike here, sticking to the right before picking up the track again for a great descent into Tarfside.

Then it's on to tarmac for a 6km spin to the foot of Mount Keen. Turning right at the

Kirkhill Forest Trail

Distance 11.5km waymarked but ungraded
Map OS Explorer 421 **Facilities** none on site

It's no surprise that Kirkhill is so popular with local riders with its swooping singletrack and a short but exciting section of jumps, camel bumps and tabletops.

Kirkhill Forest, on the northern fringe of Aberdeen, has a unique selling point among Scottish mountain bike centres. It has an airport on its doorstep, as well as a train station. The latter may be more practically useful, but the former does raise some interesting possibilities.

It has more to recommend it than this,

however. For mountain bikers in and around Aberdeen, this Forestry Commission-owned centre has become a hub and gathering point. It is the main facility in the area – and there is more in the pipeline, with plans to develop new trails.

It does need them, but what exists already is testament to the early work of the Forestry Commission and the enthusiasm of local mountain bikers. The forest contains a mix of fireroads and tracks and an increasing selection of singletrack, some man-made, some natural.

The main draw is a short fun park-style section of trail which is graded blue, but isn't quite as straightforward as this might suggest. Easily accessible from the main car park, just off the busy A96, this is a 1.6km stretch of fun park type terrain.

A gradually rising trail winds through the forest, skirting the fun park and leading to the entrance, with the radically shaped jumps, camel bumps and tabletops leading all the way back to the car park. It is short but exciting, and hopefully a taste of what's still to come.

There are other, longer-established sections of singletrack dotted around the forest. Mountain bikers are positively encouraged here, and at weekends and on evenings you will always encounter others.

As well as the myriad trails that head off the main tracks and into the forest there are two short singletrack loops, the north spur and the south spur, which can be linked up to make a good ride.

The south spur loop is close to the car park, and it makes an ideal finish to a popular and well-signposted 11.5km Forest Trail, which is predominantly on wide forest roads. It starts with a long, gradual climb before going into a brief but very exhilarating section of natural singletrack.

Not exactly downhill, but hardly flat either, this hard surfaced bit of trail is a blast into and along the side of the forest, curving around to drop you back on to the wide main track, which then cuts along the side of Tyrebagger Hill, with expansive views to the north.

From the forest road you can finish the ride with the south spur, which is a moderately technical section of singletrack that swoops and soars through the final section of forest.

Aberdeen Hill Ride

Distance **25km unmarked**
Maps **OS Explorer 406 and 421**
Facilities **none**

The highlights in this trip just keep coming, with a tight weave of singletrack trails and natural obstacles in Kingshill Wood, an exhilarating downhill from Brimmond Hill, a narrow challenging climb to Elrick Hill and the option of extending the journey to include Aberdeen's main mountain biking centre at Kirkhill.

On the northwestern edge of Aberdeen are four hills, each a good mountain biking location in itself, but it's also possible to link them up to create an epic day out.

A large park-and-ride facility at Kingswells is an ideal starting point, with a brief ride along the cyclepath adjacent to the busy A944 taking you to Kingshill Wood. After about 400m you cross this busy road, then nip through a gate and

ride up a track to access the forest.

Kingshill Wood is small but it contains a labyrinthine network of singletrack trails, many of them created simply by mountain bikers riding there. The main footpaths link up sections of singletrack that weave tightly through the forest with lots of natural obstacles, such as roots and trees, to negotiate with every turn. The route here is not waymarked: it's a case of exploring the trails as you find them. But being so small, it's difficult to get lost.

Coming out of Kingshill Wood, cross the A944 and you are back on the cyclepath, heading west again before taking a minor road to the right, in the direction of Brimmond Hill — hill number two as far as the mountain biking epic is concerned.

Hill number three, Elrick, meanwhile, is just over the other side: both of these formed part of the Freedom Lands granted to Aberdeen by Robert the Bruce in 1319.

Again, the areas around each hill are

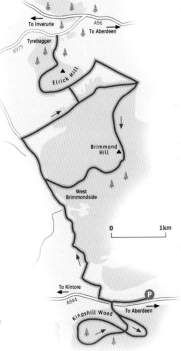

compact, but like Kingshill, they contain fantastic trails. They also form part of Aberdeen's Four Hills Walk, so both are well established places for recreation. The paths are numerous and of high quality, and they attract a lot of walkers and runners: mountain biking is a more recent activity, but do consider other users at all times.

Brimmond Hill is best tackled from the Elrick Hill side – or round the back, as you approach it by road from Kingshill Wood. The road curls round the hill, which is to your right: take the first right turn onto a road that climbs sharply to the Brimmond car park. From here, a steep singletrack rises alongside a road up to the TV masts, where the trail peters out. Then it's briefly back on tarmac to the war memorial at the top.

There's now a choice of paths, but they all give a cracking descent on narrow singletrack, passing through gorse bushes (scrapes likely) bouncing down drop-offs, heading around West Brimmondside, before eventually coming out on the road you approached by.

Then it's a case of retracing your tyre-tracks almost as far as the Brimmond car park, but turning left before then to head into Elrick Hill Country Park. The paths here are good for mountain biking, with some technical sections, too.

A particular highlight on Elrick Hill is a trail no wider than a mountain bike tyre which takes the most direct route up the heather-clad hill from Tyrebagger.

It's difficult but ultimately rewarding.

However, this climb is best tackled on the way back to Kingswells, after a visit to the fourth and final hill: Kirkhill Forest.

Kirkhill is the main mtb centre serving Aberdeen and it is described on page 68, but it's a perfect complement to the other three hills for those who want to make a (very full) day of it.

The Highlands and Islands are renowned the world over for the mountains, water and wilderness that make this an environment pretty much akin to paradise for anyone with an interest in the outdoors.

Mountain biking is up there at the top of the list, though the experience, in many places, could hardly contrast more with what you will find on the man-made trails of the 7Stanes centres in the south of Scotland, and offers riders more opportunity to make their own adventure.

However, this area does boast man-made trails too – most famously at Fort William, in the shadow of Britain's highest mountain and also home to the Mountain Bike World Cup. This is an event that has put the Highland town on the world map of mountain biking, but the quality of the trails – and the famous downhill track – also do their bit.

At Lochgilphead, in Argyll, are singletrack trails that would not be out of place at any 7Stanes centre, sharing much in terms of quality of design and construction, and offering a similarly exhilarating riding experience. The same can be said for the Black Isle, where the Learnie Red Rock Trails include a mixture of flowing red- and technically challenging black-graded trails.

Different again – but every bit as good – are the trails in Contin Forest, near the spa town of Strathpeffer, with a labyrinth of tight, natural singletrack.

And from the sublime to the more sublime, the islands of Harris and Skye have awesome trails and tracks that you are unlikely to share with too many others. There are also plenty of long-distance routes – Ullapool, Dunkeld and the Trossachs are included in this section – to test your stamina.

Highlands & Islands

Trossachs Lochs and Glens

Distance **47km unmarked**

Maps **OS Landranger 51 and 57**

Facilities **Pubs, shops, toilets in Callander and Strathyre, shop in Lochearnhead**

This is a classic circuit which climbs into the Trossachs with some technical singletrack, a river crossing and a dramatic mix of open hill and woodland.

It's an old-style Scottish route in every sense, since it takes in high glens, singletrack trails, rocks, burns and heather, with a strong sense of history evoked by the fact that it heads deep into Rob Roy country, even passing the legendary outlaw's grave in Balquhidder towards the end.

The ride starts from the east shore of Loch Lubnaig after following the main A84 road north. Opposite the second car park as you head up the side of the loch, take the forest road which rises immediately and steeply.

Before cutting across the lower slopes of Beinn Bhreac and Beinn Each, there's a T-junction, where you should turn left to continue climbing: it eventually brings you to the edge of the forest where a gate leads on to open hill.

The path deteriorates at this point or, to put it another way, it turns into technical singletrack, which continues for around 6km, until Glenample farm. There are numerous bogs and a tight, rocky path to negotiate, but it provides excellent riding with no room for a loss of concentration.

There is also no real chance of taking a wrong turning up here, since it is the only trail – even if it is hard to follow in places – for around 9km.

Up on the slopes of the glen it's decidedly Rob Roy territory, which, as Walter Scott observed, was ideal for his purpose, being 'broken up into narrow

valleys, the habitable part of which bore no proportion to the huge wilderness of forest, rocks and precipices', and not much has changed in the centuries since.

Winding down the narrow glen, 360m up, you are surrounded by some spectacular scenery. Finally you descend to the Burn of Ample, which is rideable, depending on how high the water is. The boulders on the riverbed don't make it easy, exactly, but taken at speed it can be done.

From here it's a gentle downhill all the way to Loch Earn, where you join National Route 7 (signposted) alongside the A84 to Balquhidder and the Kingshouse Hotel. Turning here on to a small and unassuming stretch of singletrack takes you up to the modest grave of one of Scotland's best known historical figures, Rob Roy.

From Balquhidder you head further south, crossing the bridge over the River Balvag, and then burling along great singletrack roads that run through dense woodland. Passing through the village of Strathyre, with its shops and pubs, and then you're back off road, still following Route 7 as it climbs up the hillside, with spectacular views down Loch Lubnaig. Steep switch-backs take you down to the lochside, and a ride around the foot of the loch brings you back to the start.

It has a bit of everything this ride: a long climb on forest roads, followed by a seriously challenging ride through Glen Ample, finished with extended sections on tarmac. But it's in a spectacular area of Scotland, and the smooth roads can be extremely welcome after such a tough slog over high ground.

Lochgilphead Fire Tower Trail

Distance **14km waymarked (Red with Black sections)** Map **OS Explorer 358**
Facilities **None on site. Bike shop/hire, pubs, shops, toilets in Lochgilphead**

Hair-raising drop-offs, rolling North Shore, murderous climbs, water splashes and amazing views, it's no wonder Lochgilphead is on top of the world when it comes to mountain biking. Just don't look down.

The Argyll town of Lochgilphead is one of the more recent hotspots for mountain biking in Scotland, but its rapidly increasing popularity is no surprise given the work that has gone on to build trails and the enthusiasm there is for the sport in the area.

These trails, which are outstanding, are just one part of the equation, however. The new Fire Tower Trail at Lochgilphead can also boast stunning views across this ruggedly beautiful area, taking in a large part of the west coast and some of the Inner Hebridean islands, including Islay and Jura.

It all starts with a lengthy climb from Achnabreck Forestry Commission Scotland car park. This involves a long haul up forest road to the start of the singletrack: a section going by the name Twisted Fire Starter, with a little optional loop known as Fire Tower. It's the highest point of the trail and, indeed, for miles around, and it feels like the top of the world: it's a fantastic vantage point for looking out over Jura,

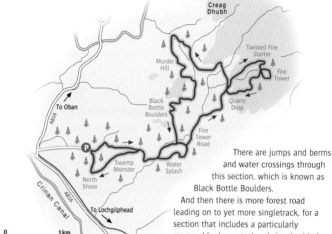

Scarba and the Corryvreckan.

Negotiating Fire Tower, it gets a bit technical: there is a vertigo-inducing drop-off coming down from the ridge, but it's rideable (just don't look down), and the trail continues to flow downhill with a very steep section – the optional black-graded Quarry Drop – taking you back to the forest road.

A fireroad descent now brings you onto a singletrack loop that ends with a leg-achingly steep climb which requires the granny ring and a serious effort to maintain any momentum at all. Not surprisingly, this one is known as Murder Hill.

The next stretch of singletrack has a more natural feel, with slightly wider trails interspersed with man-made singletrack.

There are jumps and berms and water crossings through this section, which is known as Black Bottle Boulders.

And then there is more forest road leading on to yet more singletrack, for a section that includes a particularly memorable descent, the obviously titled Water Splash, which is steep and fast with a jump positioned metres before a big bermed corner. Just beyond the bend lies a river. The stakes are, therefore, high: if you mess the jump up, you'll land in it.

Another stretch of forest road takes you to the final bit of singletrack, which is also a descent. This heads through Swamp Monster and on to some well-constructed North Shore. It's not too high or narrow, though it does thin out in places and doesn't follow a straight line. After this, a brief section of downhill singletrack spits you back out on the forest road for a short climb back up to the car park.

Work continues at Lochgilphead, and there are some ambitious plans for the area, but the Fire Tower Trail is a brilliant addition to Scotland's mountain biking offering.

Fort Bill and Cow Hill

Distance **11km unmarked**
Map **OS Explorer 392** Facilities **Bike shop/
hire, pubs, shops, toilets in Fort William**

**Reached easily from Fort William, Cow
Hill is a great place for a short blast
with a steep ascent and open views
before swooping down to Glen Nevis.**

On the approach to Fort William a
rounded lump of a hill looms up behind the
town. It catches people by surprise, since
Fort William, as everyone knows, stands in
the shadows of Britain's highest mountain,
Ben Nevis.

This, patently, is not Ben Nevis. It looks
barely 300m, never mind 1344m. And that's
because it isn't the Ben; it's Cow Hill, high
enough to obscure Ben Nevis from this
angle but not to fool anyone – surely – into
thinking that it is Britain's highest mountain.

Cow Hill is, however, an excellent place
for mountain biking. A path that skirts
around the lower slopes, just above the
town, winds around the back, climbing
to a decent height – at the path's highest
point there is also an out-and-back trail to
the summit for those interested in extending
the ride – before dropping back into Glen
Nevis by way of a new multi-use path
that is ideal for mountain biking. This is a
circular ride that, best of all, uses not one
inch of tarmac.

From the Braveheart car park in Glen
Nevis, a new path leads back towards Fort
William, cutting around the back of town
with spectacular views across Loch Linnhe.
Until recently, some 'urban orienteering' was
required to re-join the route, but a new link
path climbs to what is known locally
as the Saltire Rock (so-called because

there's a Saltire painted on it) high above Fort William.

A left turn here takes you across the front of Cow Hill, eventually joining Peat Track, which ducks around the back of the hill. Now Fort William is on your left, but hidden by the slopes, and you are climbing on a steep, unrelenting and fairly rough path, with some loose stones.

At the highest point, another path leads off to the left and the summit, but if you carry straight on you come to a 'junction': straight on is an 'Alpine-style' descent back to the car park; right is the new path.

Though it's advertised as 'multi-use', this path is easily as good as many dedicated mountain biking trails, and it looks and rides far more

like a biking trail than a footpath. A little wider than most singletrack, it swoops down the hill, bending and undulating – there are jumps and camel bumps, some of which can catch you unawares – all the way to the glen and the car park.

Potentially it is very fast, and this prompts a note of caution. Since it is intended as a multi-use path, there is every chance that it will be shared by walkers: indeed, Cow Hill is a very popular place for walkers, particularly on summer evenings, since it can be accessed so easily from Fort William.

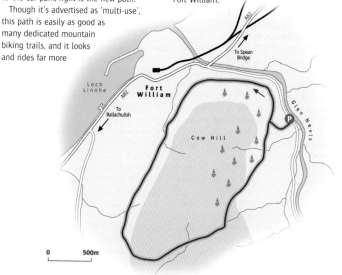

The Witch's Trails

Distance **15km waymarked (Red and Black)** Map OS Explorer 392
Facilities **Bike hire, café, toilets, bike wash**

Set in the shadow of Ben Nevis, Fort William's Witch's Trails have everything that you would expect from a World Cup cross-country course, with gnarly singletrack, boardwalk and river crossings.

Fort William is now established as one of the world's foremost mountain biking destinations, owing its good name to the success of the Mountain Bike World Cup, which was first held in 2002.

That first World Cup was the catalyst for the construction of the Aonach Mor Downhill Track – acknowledged as one of the best and toughest downhill courses in the world. And the following year's World Cup, which saw the introduction of cross-country racing, led to the construction of a world class cross-country course. The return each year of the World Cup ensures that the course is

well maintained, and regularly improved.

There are now also 'Taster Trails' by the Nevis Range car park, graded green, blue, red and black, with North Shore and other technical features on short loops which are ideal for beginners.

Known as the The Witch's Trails, the main cross-country course at the Nevis Range is where the world's top riders do battle every year. It is designed for racing, with sections of forest road to allow for overtaking, but it was also built with enjoyment in mind. The singletrack is rocky and gnarly in places, with technical features, river crossings and several hundred metres of boardwalk, but it is great to ride, and being on the slopes of Aonach Mor, in the shadow of Ben Nevis, it is also in a stunning setting.

Like the downhill track, The Witch's Trails are accessed from the Nevis Range ski centre car park. Follow the Witch's Trails signs to the first section of singletrack, a small loop that starts just metres from the car park, climbing up a steep, rocky trail which turns back on itself and plunges

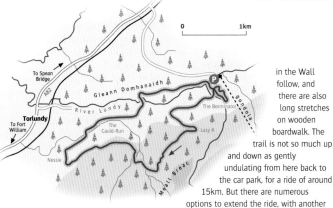

in the Wall follow, and there are also long stretches on wooden boardwalk. The trail is not so much up and down as gently undulating from here back to the car park, for a ride of around 15km. But there are numerous options to extend the ride, with another popular event – 10 Under the Ben – using a course of 16km, some of it on The Witch's Trails, all of it based in Leanachan Forest.

down to the forest road, via The Berminator, which is fast and, as the name suggests, packs in several berms and jumps.

Then it's back on to the forest road and a steady climb before the Big Up, a torturously steep climb that leads to the next bit of singletrack: Lazy K. Then there's a climb up to the entrance of Blue Crane – the highest point of the course – and a more technical downhill section that ends with the Bomb Hole.

But the most technical feature comes in about 2km, after Ridge Run and at the end of the steep Cackle descent. Nessie, with a skull and crossbones sign denoting danger at the entrance to Cackle, is a very steep and rocky descent that curls like a 'monster's' tail to drop you back out on forest road.

After about 100m it's back on to singletrack, more level and rooty now, before a fast-flowing river crossing, though this is optional: there is also a bridge.

The Cauld-Run, Rock 'n' Roll – which has you riding over a collapsed wall – and Hole

And then of course there is the downhill track, which has won a succession of plaudits and awards from the top riders, who have consistently voted it the best on the World Cup circuit. Dropping down the side of Aonach Mor, it plummets 550m in just 2.6km and, with its huge drop-offs, rock steps and jumps, it is one of the longest and toughest in the world. The access to the track – a 15-minute ride in a Nevis Range gondola – is pretty spectacular too.

The World Cup downhill track is not outwith the capabilities of those who can manage black trails fairly competently. But you might want to take it cautiously. It can thus take anything from four to 20 minutes to complete, but the important thing is to have the right bike. A full-suspension downhill bike is essential, as is a full-face helmet and padding – all of which can be rented locally.

Black Isle Learnie Red Rock Trails

Distance **20km waymarked (Red with Blue and Black sections)**
Map **OS Explorer 432** Facilities **Bike hire, pub, shop in Cromarty**

For a full-on mountain biking experience with man-made singletrack, skills loop and jump park on one side and a weave of intricate black-graded trails on the other, it doesn't get much better than the Learnie Red Rock Trails.

A gem on Scotland's mountain biking map, the Learnie Red Rocks mountain bike centre sits amid the picturesque scenery of the Black Isle, just north of Inverness. It contains a mix of man-made and natural trails and they complement each other well to provide a fantastic riding experience.

It is a centre of two halves, or two forests separated by a singletrack road. On one side, based on Callachy Hill, where there's a car park and skills loop, there are new, man-made trails with the best features of this type of terrain – jumps, berms and tabletops – all on a decent surface.

The other side, which is graded black, utilises some of the trails that have been established over the years by local mountain bikers: these are natural-style trails that twist and weave around the trees, providing a completely different challenge and a full test of your bike handling skills.

0   500m

Put together, the two halves create the Red Rocks ride. The skills loop and early sections are suitable for novices or the less fit: one blue-graded trail situated entirely on Callachy Hill, and using the man-made singletrack, measures around 8km. A jump park close to the car park also provides an introduction to some more technically challenging mountain biking.

The car park and trail head lie in woodland east of the A832 Rosemarkie to Cromarty road. To kick off the Red Rocks ride, there's a sublime ascent that curls for 1.2km beneath the high, swaying larches as it makes its gradual climb.

Then there's a brief excursion on fireroad to reach the top of a 1.5km downhill section with big berms, jumps and tabletops. This can form one of the shorter rides, since it leads you back to close to the car park, but another singletrack ascent takes you up and out of the first forest to the singletrack road between the two halves of this centre.

Here, you're on to trails that are completely different in character: the first part is downhill and cuts through dense forest on trails that have been upgraded

and improved to International Mountain Bicycling Association (IMBA) specifications.

There are many examples of ingenuity in Learnie: wooden tracks over fallen trees, hand-crafted drop-offs and step-ups. As you'd expect, there are also a lot of roots and other natural obstacles to negotiate.

The trail now heads uphill – weaving tightly through the forest as it takes anything but a direct line – and around a working quarry at the furthest point, where there is a North Shore section of around 50m. The climbs tend to be short and intricate, technical rather than leg-busting. They are fiddly, though, so foot-dabbing is difficult to avoid for all but the most skilled riders.

Everyone who visits Learnie seems impressed by the variety offered by the mix of new and old trails, with a common description being that it provides both a fun and full-on experience.

Contin Trails at Strathpeffer

Distance **16km waymarked**
Maps **OS Explorer 431 and 437**
Facilities **Bike shop/hire, pubs, shops, café, toilets in Strathpeffer**

The mtb experience in Contin Forest is full of surprises, with high rocky ridges and plenty of natural obstacles to keep things nice and challenging.

Though long established as a place for mountain biking, being used by local riders and also as a popular venue for races, Contin could still be described as the Highlands' best kept secret.

Not for long, though. For a number of years the only way to negotiate your way

around the forest was to visit Square Wheels, the cycle shop in Strathpeffer, where you would pick up your map, describing the 16km cross-country ride in all its glory. Then would come the challenge of finding your way around.

But things are changing. The local mountain bikers are now formally recognised by Forestry Commission Scotland as an official user group, which means they are responsible for maintaining and waymarking the trails.

Purists need not fear. There may now be signs to follow instead of a map, but Contin has lost none of its charm. And 'charm' is one of the best words to sum up trails that, in many places, use the existing landscape and all its natural obstacles – the big roots, fallen trees and rocky outcrops – quite ingeniously.

If anything gets in the way – big, rocky outcrops being a good example – the solution of the mountain bikers who pioneered the Contin Trails is simple: just go over the top. This leads to some fairly technical riding over high rocky ridges, with decent-sized jumps and/or drop-offs.

Work is being done, though, to upgrade some of the boardwalks that carry riders over boggy areas. But this is to make it safer rather than to smooth out Contin's rough edges.

From the Contin car park there's a long climb on forest road, though there are steep, technical singletrack climbs that cut out a couple of the hairpin bends in the road. Thereafter, it's singletrack virtually all the way: the linking sections on forest road are relatively brief.

'Natural' is the word that most use to describe the trails in Contin. Similar to Drumlanrig, in Southern Scotland, they have been created mainly by mountain bikers simply riding there, finding the best – or most interesting – lines through the trees, and up and down the hillside. You are kept on your toes, since you never know what's going to appear around the next corner: the trail could go up, down or back on itself. It's constantly changing.

One of the events held at Contin is the Strathpuffer, a 24-hour race held in the depths of the Scottish winter. This uses a course that varies slightly from the 16km cross-country, with longer sections on forest roads, which is understandable given that so much of the race is held in pitch blackness. The Strathpuffer course is also mapped, so it can be ridden by anyone who might be thinking about attempting Scotland's toughest mountain bike race.

85

Ullapool to Bonar Bridge

Distance **55km unmarked (each way)**
Maps **OS Landranger 19, 20 and 21**
Facilities **Pubs, shops, cafés, toilets in
Ullapool and Bonar Bridge. Bunkhouse, B&Bs
and hostel in and around Bonar Bridge**

**The long-distance ride from Ullapool on
the northwest coast to Bonar Bridge on
the east takes you through such
splendid scenery that you won't mind
doing the route in reverse the next day.**

This enjoyable coast-to-coast route may
not be consistently technical, but what it
lacks in that department it makes up for in
other ways. It is just long enough to
provide a nice challenge: namely,
riding one way
one day and
back the next.

At around
110km of largely
off-road riding, with
no real break or
shelter anywhere

along its length, short of wild camping or
bothying, it a challenge that demands a
high level of fitness, but is well worth
the effort.

Following mainly fireroads and farm
tracks, the main appeal of this ride is the
distance that you cover and the superb
scenery you take in on the way. It is worth
taking your time when you ride it to
appreciate the splendour of this corner of
Northern Scotland.

Starting from the picturesque fishing
village of Ullapool, on the northwest coast,

the route gives an immediate climb on steep singletrack over the hill directly above town. Keep your eyes down, though, and you are rewarded by excellent views across Loch Broom as you toil up and over.

This is followed by a rocky descent to Loch Achall, where you begin your trek east. Here the track is well surfaced and mostly flat for the length of Glen Achall, but it's not long after the East Rhidorroch Lodge buildings that the track climbs hard on a loose surface up and over to Loch an Daimh.

Marked on OS maps as a single dotted line, the trail here is in fact full track width, but it can get very rocky and technical in places, not to mention wet when the weather is against you. Pick your way carefully, and don't take any bends too fast as the track occasionally has a tendency to drop away into a jumble of rocks before you can reach for the brake levers.

Pass the bothy at Knockdamph (this can be an emergency shelter if needed) and continue down into Glen Einig. Just 500m

after Duag Bridge be careful to watch for the track climbing up on your right: this is easily missed as it is a lot less used than the main track, although both are marked as the same on most maps.

This climbs over yet another hill before dropping you into Strath Cuileannach, where the track improves and whisks you along the floor of the peaceful glen.

At Croick, the track becomes singletrack road and remains that way for the rest of the journey, but since this is a road less travelled, it is no great hardship to be clicking up through the gears and cruising through the small villages that line the route down to the coast.

Just before the Dornoch Firth, at the small village of Cornhill, take a right turn which brings you over to the main A836 road into Bonar Bridge on the Kyle of Sutherland. Get into town, get into a B&B or bunkhouse (the youth hostel at the stately Carbisdale Castle is also just up the road at Culrain) and put your feet up – you have to do it all again tomorrow.

Going Wild in Morar

Distance 18km unmarked
Map OS Explorer 398 **Facilities** Pubs, shops, cafés, toilets in Mallaig, bunkhouse in Tarbet

Morar in the West Highlands makes for an adventurous summertime route on which forbidding descents and exposed ledges are just two of the challenges.

This is not just a great mountain bike ride, it's also one of Scotland's most novel and logistically challenging – and it is certainly memorable. It starts with a journey by sea from Mallaig to a tiny settlement in the Rough Bounds, an area known for its wild and inhospitable terrain.

Tarbet is a tiny bay on North Morar, with no access by road. It was once a busy fishing port, but now contains just three buildings: two homes and an old church, now a bunkhouse. But it is connected to the coastal Road to the Isles by a thin ribbon of a path that skirts the north side of Loch Morar, passing abandoned settlements on an exhilarating and challenging mountain bike ride back to the (relative) bustle of Mallaig.

There is a ferry from Mallaig that stops first at Inverie, home to the Old Forge, the UK's most remote mainland pub, on the Knoydart peninsula, a place often referred to as 'mainland Scotland's last wilderness', and then at Tarbet. A chartered boat might be persuaded to stop off at Inverie for lunch or one of the Old Forge's famous coffees, but otherwise remain on the ferry and clamber on to the tiny jetty at Tarbet – with

mountain bikes, this is a challenge in itself – to begin the ride.

From the bay there's immediately a torturously steep climb up a rough, rocky path. It is as Tarbet recedes into the distance that you begin to appreciate just how wild these lands are.

The suitability of the path for mountain biking depends largely on the season and the weather: it is not recommended in winter (when, in any case, there are no scheduled ferries) or when it is wet. But in dry weather it is potentially one of Scotland's most rewarding rides. The path veers up steep, rocky inclines and down forbidding-looking descents, and even in summer some of the early parts of the ride will be negotiable on bike only by the most competent and confident bike handlers.

With Tarbet behind you, Loch Morar hoves into view, surrounded by towering, steeply banked mountains. The path is on the side of one such mountain, and in parts the

slope down to the water – Britain's deepest freshwater loch – is treacherously steep. In places you feel that you are hugging the hillside, leaning into it to avoid the pull of gravity, all of which adds to the exhilarating quality of this ride. But suffice to say that it is not for the faint of heart.

It is a ride of two halves. The first half will probably, for all but the best bike handlers, involve a little bit of pushing after the initial climb up from Tarbet: in places it is just too rocky and gnarly to tackle by bike. But the second half is more open, more level and it is a joy to ride: this is natural singletrack riding at its very best.

The off-road route finishes with a signpost pointing back the way to Tarbet – 11km and another world away. By road it is approximately 7km, bypassing the village of Morar at the west end of the loch with its silver sands and views out over the Small Isles, to return to Mallaig at the end of the historic Road to the Isles.

89

Sligachan on Skye

Distance **50km unmarked**
Map **OS Landranger 32**
Facilities **Hotel and campsite (with toilets and showers) at Sligachan**

This fantastic ride cuts between the Red and the Black Cuillin mountain ranges, with big climbs, technical challenges and hair-raising descents.

The Isle of Skye occupies an important place in the imagination of all hillwalkers and climbers, chiefly because the razor-edge Cuillin ridge provides such a daunting challenge. But it is a tough place for mountain biking, too, with the very demanding Sligachan route surely able to claim its title as the equivalent of the Cuillin ridge for mountain bikers.

The feeling of satisfaction – and relief – in finishing this ride, however, is immense.

It takes you through quite incredible scenery, from Sligachan through a mountain landscape that could be Alpine, with jagged peaks dominating the skyline, intercut by deep glens that funnel down to a vast, sparkling sea. It is, in short, a quite awe-inspiring place to find yourself on a mountain bike.

A good place to start is the Sligachan Hotel, where you should cross the old bridge (closed to traffic). Straight ahead through the gate, a path climbs into the distance and as you tackle this it quickly becomes apparent why this ride might earn the title as one of – if not the – toughest in the country.

It isn't the relative length of the route but the terrain that provides the real challenge. There are rocks – thousands of them – and they come in all shapes and sizes from small, loose stones right through to boulders. It makes for tricky riding, with the most technical section following a path that skirts the foot of classic peaks such as Sgurr Nan Gillean and Blà Bheinn (Blaven).

This part of the ride takes you along the floor of the glen towards the sea at Camasunary: it lasts a whopping 15km and can prove tricky. Boulders, drainage cuttings, steep bedrock climbs and sharp descents that have you leaning back, holding on for dear life – all of these feature here. Inevitably there are some sections that are better tackled on foot, but around 90 per cent of this route is rideable – as long as you have the confidence to go for it over one or two of the more forbidding-looking sections.

From the bottom of the glen you hit the coast, with Camasunary bothy – on the far (west) side of Loch na Creitheach from the path – a good place for shelter and a rest. There's a brief spell on pleasant farm tracks before the climb out of the glen, where the surface is dominated by loose stones that can create difficulties. But there's a great descent on the other side, where the loose stones only add to the enjoyment.

A spell on the B8083 comes as a welcome relief. It doesn't last long, though. The next technical off-road section to Luib takes you through a narrow glen. It can be quite waterlogged, with bogs and burns to

negotiate. Luib offers another opportunity for some rest and recuperation before it's back on to the road and around the coast to Sligachan. This is a fantastically tough but spectacular and exhilarating ride to challenge and reward the fittest, hardiest mountain bikers.

Reinigeadal Rollercoaster

Distance **20km unmarked**
Map **OS Landranger 14** Facilities **Pubs,
shops, café, bunkhouse in Tarbert, hostel
in Reinigeadal**

**This awe-inspiring route starts in Tarbert
on mountainous North Harris, which can
be reached by ferry direct from Uig on
the Isle of Skye or from the mainland
via the Ullapool-Stornoway ferry (there's
also an airport in Stornoway on Lewis).**

Part of the Hebridean archipelago, Harris
contains mountain biking that has been
described as the very best in the UK.

The reason is simple – the trails are
superb. Perfect singletrack that stretches
across rugged and remote hills, frequently
only around 30cm wide, with a tough, gritty
surface which is ideal for riding on. There is
a massive network of such paths on Harris –
many of them thus far undiscovered by
mountain bikers.

From the island's main village, Tarbert,
you follow the narrow Scalpay road
eastwards for about 2km before the trail
branches off to the left, dropping steeply
down towards a lochside. Follow this trail as
it weaves through outcrops of rock over
terrain that in places is worn down to
bedrock, providing one or two technical
challenges. As it climbs, the singletrack
narrows some more to reach the head of the
glen and a cairn, a good place to stop and
admire the breathtaking mountain views.

Then it's back in the saddle to descend by
a grassy trail, soon turning to hacked
Harris singletrack, to the road. This gives an
easygoing 1.5km along Loch Màraig before
the grinding climb up an impossibly steep
stretch of tarmac. Finally the road
plummets back down to the start of another
section of trail bound for Tarbert. Right at
the start of this trail is Reinigeadal, a
charming little village with a tiny

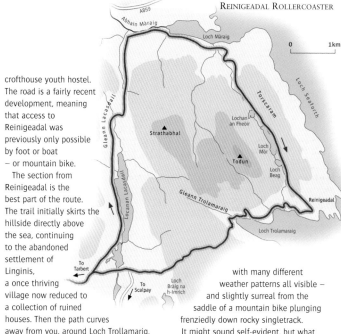

crofthouse youth hostel. The road is a fairly recent development, meaning that access to Reinigeadal was previously only possible by foot or boat – or mountain bike.

The section from Reinigeadal is the best part of the route. The trail initially skirts the hillside directly above the sea, continuing to the abandoned settlement of Linginis, a once thriving village now reduced to a collection of ruined houses. Then the path curves away from you, around Loch Trollamarig.

There's a steep climb up from the bay, before the trail drops down to yet another bay. Then the path cuts, so steeply it looks almost vertical, up the other side of the glen, zigzagging through the heather.

A wooden footbridge at the foot of a fantastic twisty, gravelly and technical descent leads into this climb. Spectacular though the climb is, it is sadly too steep to ride. Shouldering the bike and trekking up the hill is the only option – it's tough going.

But a great descent takes you back down to Tarbert, with stunning views across to the neighbouring islands and the sea, often with many different weather patterns all visible – and slightly surreal from the saddle of a mountain bike plunging frenziedly down rocky singletrack.

It might sound self-evident, but what makes this route so pleasurable is the rideability of many of the trails. With the exception of the major climb, there are extended sections of singletrack that simply demand to be ridden: and you can do so comfortably, without dabbing feet or even climbing out of the saddle, save perhaps for the odd rocky stretch, just to keep things (even more) interesting.

In places the singletrack stretches tantalisingly ahead: a narrow ribbon of gravel trail winding its way through a remote and spectacular landscape. No wonder Harris is so highly rated by those who've ridden there.

More Harris Highs

Distance **39km unmarked**
Map **OS Landranger 14** Facilities **Pubs, shops, café, bunkhouse in Tarbert**

The Clisham on North Harris is the highest peak in the Outer Hebrides so its not surprising that a route which skirts both this and its neighbour Uisgneabhal Mor is going to be tough.

This wilderness route on Harris uses the same ancient crofters' paths that our Reinigeadal trail (p92) follows. Only this one takes you a lot further, where no roads dare go.

It is a long day in the saddle, with three strenuous climbs of quite exceptional hills and passes, but it rewards you with a real wilderness feel, some stunning singletrack trails and every likelihood that you will not meet another soul on the off-road sections.

The path, although little used these days, has remained in superb condition through the years. While it still has its firm base and is

built up out of any boggy areas, it has grown over with a layer of lush green grass for much of the climb out of Gleann Langadail. This makes some of the trail a bit of a slog, but you are more than rewarded with the singletrack past Loch Chleistir, which will just take your breath away if the weather is right. If the weather is wrong, this could be one long section of exposed hillside trail.

The only downside you could assign this route is the amount of road you see it following on the map. Don't forget, though, this is Harris. The roads here are a pleasure to ride. After battling over so much off-road it could just come as a pleasant break and an opportunity to cast your eye out over the sea and surrounding hills. On the trail, meanwhile, you will only have eyes for the singletrack.

The route begins just north of Aird a'Mhulaidh on the A859 between Tarbert and Stornoway. On a tight right hand bend, crossing the Abhainn Bhioigadail, take the

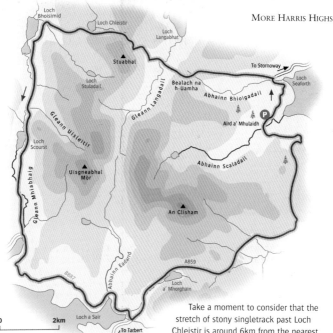

0 2km

wide singletrack climbing west away from the road. This deteriorates in places and can be quite wet, but is always fun to ride as it climbs up to the Bealach na h-Uamha.

Beyond the bealach, a stony descent takes you into the glen where you are greeted by the sight of what was the bridge over the Abhainn Langadail. Bridge supports either side of the river are all that is left, so there is no option but to wade across.

The grassy climb on the old crofters' path continues here, and it can be quite energy sapping – but just think of the beautiful trail that awaits you at the top of the ascent.

Take a moment to consider that the stretch of stony singletrack past Loch Chleistir is around 6km from the nearest road as the crow flies, so this wouldn't be the best place to have an accident.

The descent is over all too soon and you pop out at a fishing hut in Gleann Mhiabhaig before a pleasurable scoot down the well-kept and fast flowing estate track through the glen.

Emerging at the bottom you are on to tarmac for the blast back round to the Tarbert road. There is plenty to look out for even here, including the unexpected sight of an immaculate tennis court built into the hillside, or the remnants of the old whaling station, just before you join the main road to take you back to the start.

Links

Southern Scotland

7stanes.gov.uk
thehubintheforest.co.uk (Glentress)
buccleuch.com (Drumlanrig)
ae-up.co.uk (Forest of Ae uplift service)

Central Scotland

carronvalley.org.uk
arranbikeclub.com
arranadventure.com
stirlingbikeclub.org.uk

North-east Scotland

mountainbikers.org.uk (Cairngorms)
rothiemurchus.net
moraymountainbikeclub.co.uk
forestry.gov.uk/wolftrax (Laggan)
glenmorelodge.org.uk
badaguish.org

Highlands and Islands

himba.org.uk (Highlands)
ridefortwilliam.co.uk
fortwilliamworldcup.co.uk
squarewheels.biz (Strathpeffer)
strathpuffer.co.uk
10undertheben.com
midargyllcycleclub.co.uk (Lochgilphead)

General

cycling.visitscotland.com
forestry.gov.uk/scotland
mountain-bike-scotland.com
cyclingscotland.org
scottishsport.co.uk
mb7.com
imba.com
trailscotland.com
sustrans.org.uk